BREAKING THROUGH

TOM

I wish you
His peace in
breaking through
several walls
this year

Don Osgood

Don Osgood

BREAKING THROUGH

Fleming H. Revell Company
Old Tappan, New Jersey

"Elements of Effective Management Assessment Process," by William P. Densmore. Copyright © 1984 by William P. Densmore; all rights reserved; reproduced by permission of the author.

"How to Retire at Thirty-five" adapted from an advertisement created by Marstellar (now HCM) 866 Third Ave, New York, N. Y. 10022.

Library of Congress Cataloging-in-Publication Data
Osgood, Don.
  Breaking through.

  1. Employee motivation.   2. Executives—Psychology.
3. Professional employees—Psychology. I. Title.
HF5549.5.M63084   1986   658.3'14   86-494
ISBN 0-8007-1472-5

Contents

How to Get the Most Out of This Book

Organizations of all kinds—profit making, not-for-profit, governmental and religious—are faced with a common dilemma. Employees decline in productivity and vision, causing personal grief, physical burnout, and massive corporate expense. But there are important incidents of individual revitalization, a new burst of commitment and productivity that changes the organization as well as the individual. The time has come to focus on this to foster a new wave of organizational productivity and individual worth at work.

Breaking Through is a rare opportunity to learn how to revitalize experienced employees and to become personally renewed at the same time. You can do both, but you've got to be willing to be both a leader, with an eye toward what will work in your organization, and a discerning person who wants new ideas and approaches you can use for yourself. This book is written for you, as both a professional leader and as a renewable individual, because you can't be one without the other.

With thirty years in IBM, most of them in management development, including eight years at the international corporate level, I found a need for a book that shows how professional vitality can be renewed in individuals, and how individuals can revitalize an organization. This book will help you do that by helping you recognize seven vital attitudes that will make or break your career.

Breaking Through will go to the source of vitality and productivity—individual heart attitude, an almost unrecognized concept in business.

Get ready for a different approach to individual motivation based on the fact that productivity never exists without personal vitality. Consider the actual stories of revitalization in companies such as IBM (where I've changed the employees' names) and DuPont, through a program called New Perspectives, then think of this: vitality is a product of what you expected in the past, what you find happening now and what you really want to happen in the future. As you read, look for the importance of the gap between these perceptions—how this gap affects your vitality, your motivation, and your personal productivity.

The gap between the expectations you once had for your life and the reality of what is happening now is offset by the depth of your desire for the future. When you know how to look for these gaps and how to deal with them, you can actually help people change their attitudes. You, too, can be remarkably renewed in a surprisingly short time. And you can put the process in gear with practice in using simple but sound questions, rather than intricate psychological expertise.

Breaking Through will not only show you how this has already been done, but how it can be done by typical men and women in typical organizations across the United States. It will show you how to create more vitality, productivity, and quality. We will not follow an academic approach. Personal experiences and fast-paced personal illustrations will lead you through easy-to-follow steps that you can take on both a personal level and an organizational level. That is why this book will appeal to management and non-management people alike, because everyone wants to extend personal vitality and all organizational leaders want to increase productivity. The way to do that over the long run is to reduce gaps between managers and employees. This book will help you do that—across profit, not-for-profit, governmental, and religious organizations—by the use of real experiences that apply to all these sectors of organizational life.

Can Americans rediscover the work attitudes that will help us regain our historic ability to compete? The answer is yes; we can do it one by one, and it can begin here. But to make it happen, you've got to approach this book with the resolve to recreate vitality in yourself, however alive you are now, and in your organization. You've got to have enough vision to help your corner of business America.

As you move through this book, resolve to practice an extraordinary way of life at work, guided by four purposes:

- to serve completely
- to believe wholeheartedly
- to recognize immediately
- to act decisively and creatively

Your vision will come as you read and as you apply these four revitalizing steps that can renew your organization and change the rest of your career.

Part I

Creating New Vitality in Yourself

1

Who Needs a New Start?

To every problem there is already a solution whether you know it or not.

—GRENVILLE KLEISER

When Curt's plane touched down at LaGuardia, he didn't really know what was ahead at this new school. All he knew was that he had been selected for a special program. He didn't know that the very next morning he would be saying things he never thought he would say to anyone, certainly not at a company school for professional leaders—to people he had never met.

Waiting at the baggage counter was a chauffeur. "Your limousine is at the curb, Mr. Blanchard."

Curt sank into the velvet seat of the long, dark Cadillac, wondering if there might have been a mistake.

"You *are* going to Sands Point, aren't you?"

"Yes, sir, we are. At this time of night we'll be there in less than thirty minutes."

Curt snapped on a small reading light just behind his head and slipped the invitation letter out of his suit coat to recheck the location. "Ah, Sands Point," he breathed to himself with reassurance, then scanned the letter again.

"This will be an unusual week for you," the invitation said. "You have been selected as a professional leader, and we want you to come with the full intent to become involved, rather than merely to listen. . . ." Curt's thoughts broke out in a soft spoken word. *"Involved,"* he said, looking into the darkness, trying to cut through the reason the word troubled him.

As the limousine swept quietly through a stone gate, Curt could see, in the moonlight, a castlelike building on a low hill, surrounded by ancient trees. Curt was already visually involved as he peered through the darkness. As the limousine stopped noiselessly under a portico, Curt barely remembered to pull a crumpled bill from his pocket. It was chilly as he waited outside for the door to open. He found himself repeating the word. "Involved," he said, as the door opened, revealing an old-world room and a huge, glowing fireplace fifty feet away, at the end of the room.

"Welcome," said a smiling, slender man. "We've got a little buffet for you if you're hungry."

Curt felt the fire warming the autumn chill out of his clothes as he ate. There were several quiet surprises that evening: the marble staircase, the fireplace in his room, the library.

At 8:30 the next morning, Curt was sitting in an oak-paneled room at a twenty-foot oval table, looking at twelve other men chatting quietly. *Thirteen of us,* he thought. *And I don't know anyone here.* He looked at an easel chart at the front of the room that declared:

I WILL BE SUCCESSFUL THIS WEEK IF I CAN:

- Redefine and begin to realize my personal goals where I am right now
- Increase my understanding of personal strengths and weaknesses
- Extend my personal perspective of the company and see more clearly my own role in it

As Curt finished reading the chart, a door at the front of the room opened and a silver-haired man in a blue suit walked to the head of the table and spoke.

"If we are successful together this week, we will experience the most significant program of our careers—maybe of our lives." He paused for a moment. "We are here to work together on three key issues facing the company and to reach these three personal objectives." Tapping the easel chart, he pointed to the objectives Curt had just read.

Curt reflected on his background as a marketing representative. He was a good one, with a comfortable career ahead. After fifteen years, he had become articulate, confident, and successful, with 1.5 million revenue points and a national account. His career looked like a piece of cake, yet he felt troubled by something that he had not told anyone for years—and had almost forgotten.

Now Curt tuned in to the man at the head of the table.

"This organization we belong to is yours to look at, more carefully than you have before. We want you to do something different for yourself and for the organization. We are in danger of becoming another Packard automobile company or a once-great railroad. You can't afford to let us be that, because you have twenty years or more to spend here. We are middle-aged now, you and I—and so is this company."

Curt looked around for reactions. This didn't sound like a marketing school or anything he had attended, not even the manage-

15

ment school he had attended four years ago, when he became a new manager.

The man in the blue suit was speaking again. "The three key company issues I mentioned are these." He turned on the projector and Curt read the bulleted list on the screen.

Three Key Professional Leadership Issues

- How can we motivate, revitalize, and maintain the challenge for professional employees through the experienced professional years (ten years to retirement)? What creative yet practical programs and techniques do you recommend? What reorganizing or restructuring of relationships should be done, if any?
- In a period of strong emphasis on organizational and individual productivity, what should be done to increase productivity while maintaining respect for the individual? What can be done to promote an environment of productive teamwork at the branch or department level all the way to the top?
- What functional skills, education, and experiences are needed by our experienced professionals? What do you recommend we do as an integrated employee development approach for professional sales, systems, administration, and headquarters people?

When Curt finished reading the issues he heard the man in the blue suit again.

"We'll need your recommendations on these issues. But this morning, we have some important personal work to do. We've got to overcome our cultural dishonesty, and I'm starting with me."

Suddenly Curt felt more involved as he listened to the man tell of his career mistakes, along with his successes, of his son, who had run away while he had become preoccupied with his career, of his slow slide into quiet resignation and apathy on the job when his career had slowed down. Finally, the man sat down, and Curt heard him say, "Now that I've introduced myself, I'd like to hear from you, at any level you'd like to introduce yourself. I'll be quiet until one of you speaks."

Curt listened to himself now with disbelief. He was talking to the group just as the speaker had done!

"I was a manager four years ago," Curt said quietly, "and they took me out! I hit bottom then, and I've been trying to work my way back up for four years." Curt's face showed a deep red anger now. "I nearly ruined my family. I ran out on my wife. . . ." He stopped short for a moment, uncertain, looking at each person in the room. "I became a heavy drinker. I've never resolved one burning question. *Can I become involved again?* I mean, really involved, as a manager. I'd like to show them I can make it."

It became suddenly quiet in the room as the men watched Curt's face working with emotion. There was an understanding that rarely happens between thirteen strangers. No one spoke a word. No one needed to. It was too soon for them to know, but that morning became the beginning of a powerful new vitality for the thirteen men and the beginning of a powerful vitality program for the organization.

Dan O'Rourke, another of the thirteen, had come from Tulsa as a systems engineer. He had the look of an analytical person, watching everything as though he were debugging a glitch in a software program. But he reached a turning point on Thursday of that week; it changed his career and caused him to remark later, "That experience earned me a promotion two years before I would have received it."

Ralph Kennedy, a third member of the thirteen, had come from Washington, D.C., as an instructor. This congenial-looking, gray-haired, fifty-year-old felt satisfied to live out his career in an education center. But in the early morning hours on that Friday, Ralph made a career decision that would cause him to become the company's senior marketing representative to the White House at age fifty-one.

Discovering Professional Leadership

By the time those three men returned to their organizations, they had already become professional leaders. No one had changed their titles, but that didn't matter. They were professional leaders *inside* before they became recognized by their IBM colleagues and the organization around them.

We tend to overlook the beginnings of professional leadership. We don't even think about leadership beyond the managerial level. But what if we did: What would a personal leadership attitude at the bottom do for an individual's vitality and for the productivity of an organization?

In 1967 I asked some representatives of the Southern Christian Leadership Conference to define *leadership* for me, since their organization name included the word and since Dr. Martin Luther King, Jr., had shown the world that he was a leader. I invited Dr. King to address our management school on this subject. His staff responded, "He can't do it this year, but he will be glad to next year, when he returns to the conference center." Before the next conference he was assassinated.

In the meantime, I asked Dr. King's young staff person if he would like to visit our management class to define leadership. He seemed bright, articulate, and enthusiastic. At the time I didn't know the potential of the man I asked. When I introduced Andrew Young to the group of managers, no one recognized his name, but that day we listened to the future ambassador to the United Nations and mayor of Atlanta. Instead of defining leadership, in strikingly simple and reasonable terms, he described how they selected leaders.

"When we go into a town where we feel there is racial injustice," he said, "we ask the first of three questions: 'Who in this town thinks there is a problem?' When we find a group of people who think there is a problem, we ask, 'Who thinks something ought to be done about this problem?' To those who respond, we ask the third question, 'Do *you* want to do something about the problem?' Those who do are the group from which we find our leaders."

I have never forgotten that description, because I've found that it works for any organization and any individual. It sets the groundwork for recognizing, creating, and utilizing productive leadership. We will not waste time defining *leadership*. People have been doing that for centuries, and it does little good for an individual and an organization, unless they can recognize it, multiply it, and utilize it. The organization that can will reap a harvest of productivity.

Recognizing Leadership

Leadership occurs when someone:

- knows something needs to be done
- has an idea of what he or she ought to do
- does something about it

When a person applies those three simple yet profound steps to his or her profession, on a specific job, in a specific organization, professional leadership occurs. It *always* occurs. Few people have recognized this unwritten law!

The effectiveness, intensity, and power of leadership are simply a matter of *how deeply* a person feels something needs to be done, *how profound* an idea a person has of what he or she ought to do, and *how much* the person actually does.

There is nothing magic or uncommon about leadership. Anyone can acquire it, in any walk of life and in any organization. Look again at Curt Blanchard, Dan O'Rourke, and Ralph Kennedy. Each was a unique individual who came to the point of recognizing that he had to take action in his career.

We will look more closely at Ralph Kennedy first. When Ralph reached the time for decision in his class at Sands Point, he experienced a quiet yet powerful moment. Friday morning, he knew he had to say something about his career to the other twelve members of his class. At age fifty, he felt no need to change his direction. He had arrived at the school well adjusted and happy with his place in life. But all week long, he had been encouraged to think about doing something different. On that last morning, with three minutes to crystallize his week, he reported to his colleagues, "I'm going to talk with my manager about a new direction for me. I was content to live out the rest of my career as an instructor, but that's gone now."

One year later, I looked for a graduate who could become a role model for participants at other schools just like the one Ralph Kennedy had attended. The program had remained very much alive, with a backlog of candidates eager to attend, from departments whose managers more than willingly paid the fee. Now it was time to utilize some of the professional leaders, if we could find any after a year.

I called management in Washington, D.C., and asked if they could recommend a graduate who had done something different, who could come and talk to people attending the school. The manager said, "Call Ralph Kennedy."

When I talked with Ralph, I knew he had something to say to other participants. I invited him to speak on Thursday afternoon, for an hour and a half, on what he had done as a professional leader. When Ralph arrived, he was eager to talk.

"When I left here, I knew I had to do something about my career," he told me. "I walked by my manager's office until I had the courage to walk in. 'I want to go back to the field,' I said, and to my surprise, he listened. 'All right,' he responded. 'Let's work on it.' A few weeks later, at age fifty-one, with my manager's help, I walked into the White House as IBM's senior marketing representative!"

Ralph Kennedy had taken three simple-appearing, but difficult steps, when you consider his level of comfort before attending the Sands Point experience and his age. Ralph Kennedy:

1. decided something had to be done
2. had a clear idea of what he had to do to get started
3. did it

I brought Ralph Kennedy back again and again to talk to participants, and he made a telling impact on every class.

Now let's look at Dan O'Rourke. At the end of the school, he came to me privately, after he had given his presentation on the last day. "I don't want to be a manager. And I don't want to change jobs," he said. "But I do want to be a professional leader right where I am."

"Then you've got to describe what that is," I told him. "If you are willing to write an article on what it means to be a professional leader in your branch office, I'll do what I can to get it published."

Dan went back to Tulsa and asked to give a report to his team, then to the entire branch office, on ways the branch could become more vital, more productive. Afterwards he wrote about it, and we published Dan's article in the division management magazine. I brought him into the school as a role model, and later I brought him to management schools as a teacher. The impact was strikingly effective, just as it had been with Ralph Kennedy. Dan had become a professional leader in his own department and his own branch, in the *same job*. He had pushed out the walls of his assignment. When I visited him later in Tulsa, he reported with enthusiasm, "I've been promoted to consulting systems engineer, at least two years ahead of my expectation!" The reason: he had become more productive without anyone changing his job title or his formal assignment.

A few years after his Sands Point experience, I visited Curt Blanchard, the man who had been in management before and had been so open about his desire to return to it. His career had changed remarkably. Curt had moved to another location to shed an organization stereotype that could have frozen him out of management. "I wanted to do something different," he said, now sitting in the low-key elegance of his office, impeccably appointed with contemporary walnut furniture. Behind him hung a framed oriental scene, and to his right, an oversized picture window looked out on a shimmering pond below. Curt radiated quiet success.

He had been promoted to management again, had done well, and was promoted again to another position. He spoke with confidence and warmth. "I can still feel the impact of my statement at Sands Point," he said. "And I carried away a deeper ability to understand experienced professionals. I've done a lot of counseling since Sands Point, mostly advising people to get into assignments where they did their best in the past, instead of reaching for some coveted level. I've also learned how to get the most out of experienced professionals. First, I listen carefully, to let them know I really understand them. I want them to know I trust them. Then I give them a lot of room to work out the boundaries of their job. I've seen three long-term professionals move on to managerial jobs that way."

We talked then of the importance of an organization climate that doesn't allow management to give up on the long-service employee. New vitality and greater productivity come to an organization that takes two specific steps with its people: bring in new, young talent and *at the same time* encourage old talent to do something different with their jobs, their careers, and their lives. Curt Blanchard was a living example of that as he talked. His dark blue suit, white shirt, red tie, and pocket handkerchief made a distinguished visual impact, and his words carried the wisdom of experience. "I've had a lot of help from peers who were willing to talk and managers who were willing to give me advice," he said. "Now I'm asking, 'Where to from here?' "

I could see Curt Blanchard's confident renewal and warm sensitivity as we walked through plush corridors on the way to the oak-paneled elevator. He had carried his professional leadership into managerial leadership without forgetting the importance of a powerful skill: the ability to handle success without putting distance between himself and people he speaks with.

This key skill that Curt Blanchard has acquired is also an essential ingredient of long-term organization success. It requires a clear statement, perhaps even a sign over the door of every manager's office:

> ORGANIZATIONS THAT REMAIN VITAL SHOW THEIR NEW EMPLOYEES THAT THEY ARE NEEDED. AT THE SAME TIME, THEY NEVER FORGET THE VALUE OF THEIR LONG-SERVICE EMPLOYEES. AND THEY ALWAYS GIVE BOTH A SECOND CHANCE.

Curt Blanchard got his second chance at management in IBM, and he became better the second time around. Ralph Kennedy got his second chance at a marketing job in the White House. Dan O'Rourke got his second chance right in his own branch, as a consultant to his own organization as well as a consulting systems engineer to IBM's customers. All three men are examples of many more who helped IBM's main-line marketing division move through an adjustment period when the media thought the company had lost its touch. But the seeds of new productivity had been quietly and painstakingly planted in a dual emphasis on vision and people vitality.

This emphasis spread from a reconsideration of IBM's market strategy all the way through to a renewal of hundreds of selected professionals who developed a professional leadership attitude. The reassessment of the marketing strategy paved the way for IBM to change from a high-profit, low-volume producer of large computers to a lower profit, high-volume personal-computer strategy. Separate from this strategy, while the company changed its product approach and the marketing staff waited, IBM's main-line marketing division started the experienced-employee vitalization program that Curt Blanchard, Dan O'Rourke, and Ralph Kennedy attended. It wasn't part of a specific plan that these two emphases occurred together, but a part of the culture of renewal that IBM had always fostered.

The Keys to Remotivation

Along the way, an underlying question kept appearing: What really motivates experienced employees, whether they are managers or professionals? When they lose their way, what makes them lose it?

Two surprisingly simple truths began to rise from the Sands Point experience: First, when experienced employees are given a new challenge to expand their individual roles right where they are—to do something different and constructive—they act much like new employees in their level of vitality, and they bring the added wisdom of long service to their work. When you tell an old employee that he doesn't have a brick on his head, in fact, that you are asking him to act like a professional leader, *even though he isn't sure what that is,* that person will become remotivated. Second, when you let a person know she is on the inside, rather than on the outside, waiting for someone to tell her what to do, she will respond with all the motivation of a new hire. You do this by including the professional employee in on problems of the organization that are not yet solved—the most strategic ones you can identify, as bold and far-reaching as the three key professional leadership issues Curt Blanchard, Dan O'Rourke, and Ralph Kennedy addressed at Sands Point:

1. How can we motivate, revitalize and challenge the experienced employees?
2. What should be done to increase productivity while maintaining respect for the individual?
3. What skills, education, and experiences are needed by experienced employees?

The wise management team encourages such personal growth-in-place attitudes for both young and old employees, and when they do, long-lasting motivation begins. But an honest willingness to listen, to let people express initial frustrations without penalty must also exist so that their built-in desire to perform will be released again.

You have only to listen to the statements of long-service employees before they are revitalized to know the depths of the problem that can occur and the remarkable recovery that is possible.

Inside-out, bottom-up renewal produces a quiet resurgence of professional leadership and vitality over time. This signals the very beginning of productivity renewal for an organization. Without listening to and constructively responding to its long-service employees, no organization ever remained productive for long. The statement that one can judge a society by the way it treats its old people applies squarely to business America. The young employees are watching not only how the organization treats them, but how it treats the senior employees.

This renewal doesn't apply to IBM alone or to men exclusively. In the DuPont Corporation, thirteen more professionals gathered together to experience a new perspective that shows how universal the motivation of people really is. In chapter 17 you will see how a young woman is helping the Navistar International Corporation. It can happen anywhere, with anyone. But first we need to understand the attitudes that can make or break a career or a corporation. Without them, we cannot begin to make the changes revitalization calls for.

2

**Seven
Attitudes
That
Can Make
or
Break You**

*The greatest discovery of our generation is that a
human being can alter his life by altering his attitudes.*
—WILLIAM JAMES

There are seven basic attitudes that all people go
through some time in their lives. These attitudes show
up in careers, marriages, and personal experiences. The
order they appear in is not always the same, but in one
way or another they have a marked effect on everything
a person does. They spell the difference between productivity and inactivity, between fruitful friendship and loss

of friendship, between success and failure.

Your attitudes can make or break you. They can even make the difference between good health and a life of illness. But contrary to widespread opinion, it is never too late to change your attitude and to set your career or personal life back on course. You will find an attitude barometer below that shows how attitudes often change.

Identifying Your Attitude

There are many shapes over time to an individual's attitude. That's partly due to the fact that each attitude may hide a deeper driving force that takes practice to spot. You can begin now to become more aware of your attitudes. Pick the one from those on the next pages that is most nearly yours at the moment along with those you've had over the last twelve months. Discuss them with your friends. Sometimes a person looking on can spot your attitude even more clearly than you. It's important to get honest input because you may have buried your attitude so deep that you no longer recognize it, even though it may be holding you back from a more fulfilling career or relationship. How often have you heard someone say, "He's always tripping over his ego," or, "She's like an uncoiled spring. There's no ambition left!" These comments are symptoms of one of the seven attitudes shown below. Some are positive. Some are not. Look at all seven of these attitudes, then consider yours.

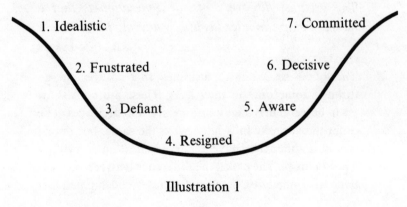

1. Idealistic
2. Frustrated
3. Defiant
4. Resigned
5. Aware
6. Decisive
7. Committed

Illustration 1

1. Idealistic, superficial. The idealistic attitude is a "new beginning" attitude, marked by high hopes and enthusiasm. Such an attitude occurs with the onset of your career or a major change in your job or life, such as marriage. People with this attitude feel they can make virtually anything work out well, because they feel they have the right talents and are in the right place at the right time.

2. Frustrated, anxious. When a person begins to see a gap between personal expectations or desires and present circumstances, worry or anxiety sets in and momentum slows down. A person may ask, *What's really going on here? Where am I heading?* This is a time of troublesome indecision brought about by a fear that things may not work out as well as expected. Sustained frustration (often from fear and indecision) brings on anxiety, and that is never motivating or productive for an organization, marriage, or an individual. Frustration becomes the breeding ground for the next attitude.

3. Defiant, angry. After experiencing frustration a person comes to a conclusion that things clearly won't work out as expected unless something definite is done. Often this happens when a person sees a wider gap between personal expectations and reality or when a long time goes by with no change in a positive direction.

When the defiant attitude occurs, fear and indecision are no longer forces. A take-charge attitude takes their place, one that says in essence, "I guess I'm going to have to make some changes here, if no one else will." Now defiance or anger sets in.

There are two levels of defiance: covert and overt. Neither is constructive, but covert defiance proves especially unproductive—even destructive—in the long run. A covert-defiant person often doesn't know that he or she is defiant and may bury personal anger for days, months, even years. Longer service employees or people married for a long time may have this attitude for many years without realizing it. This buried defiance can lead to attitude number four, *resigned.*

4. *Resigned, uninvolved.* The resigned attitude occurs when a person feels there is no longer any use in trying to change things. Often people mentally resign from their jobs or from some other commitment, such as a marriage, but they don't actually leave. Their bodies are still around, but their creative, productive spark is gone. Such people will do what is legally or socially required and little more. They stop trying to make constructive contributions and move to a more passive role. They become people who hang on or hang around saying, "What's the use?" Usually only major effort by someone else will cause change in the resigned person.

Those who have acquired a "What's the use?" attitude engage in a form of pouting or vindictiveness. There are several symptoms of this: a sudden preference for working or being alone, missed schedules or appointments, a pattern of unaccountable absence, increased drinking, irritability, or fault finding.

The resigned attitude is always serious, not only for the person who has it, but for others. It can become contagious, but the next attitude can help.

The Beginning of Change

5. *Aware, accepting.* People reach the aware or accepting attitude when they see that they must be willing to change. There is no real awareness without an honest acceptance of personal responsibility and need for personal change.

Someone else's honesty often causes personal awareness. There is always a risk here. Such honesty isn't always wanted.

Often, an individual can be brought to awareness by a statement of the real situation. For instance, a supervisor might say to an employee, "Ann, I'm worried about you. I feel that you are drifting, and I'm afraid of what this may lead to in a few months." Here's another that deals with personal feelings at home: "Harry, I have the feeling that the children and I aren't as important to you as we once were." This constructive, straightforward statement of the situation can lead to a helpful discussion if the person starting the discussion couples it with real concern for the person. Otherwise the risk of this level of honesty may be too great. Willingness to change or do something differently—whether the change involves oneself or someone else—always carries the risk of failure and possible loss of relationship. But the potential for dramatic change also exists.

We bring on the awareness attitude when we look squarely in the mirror and accept ourselves for what we are—or someone else for what he or she is. It means taking stock and accepting the possibility that nothing good will come unless change takes place. This constructive attitude sets the stage for the next one: a decisive attitude. With awareness, nothing can stop the decisive attitude from coming on like a refreshing rain—or a tidal wave of constructive activity.

6. Decisive, changing. This is an active, productive attitude. While real awareness triggers decisiveness, it doesn't happen until change is actually begun—until you actually pull the trigger.

As you take any new step, decision is born—while your foot is in the air. This exhilarating, stress-releasing attitude starts in your heart, transfers to your head, and ends in your feet and your hands.

Decisive people *consciously* do something different. Sometimes you must learn to take such action, especially if you've become too comfortable for your own good. Sometimes it is necessary to decide to do something different in a safer, smaller area of life or work before tackling a main area. Everyone wants to be decisive, unless they've been hurt too much or too often. For most people, being decisive allows new freedom. For some it is like breaking out of prison. For organizations it is the breath of vitality that pumps new vigor into the work that needs doing. But one more attitude sustains the vitality that decisiveness starts. It's called "commitment," and it's an essential part of success.

7. Committed, involved, oriented. We become committed when we don't expect perfection of our organization, our marriage, our relationship, or even ourselves, yet we want to make things work. We strive for excellence, knowing that perfection is often idealistic.

The committed attitude is not a reaction to things that are going wrong but an active, working desire to help out. There is no idealistic feeling in this attitude. No magic words guarantee that everything will turn out all right. Rather, there is a practical understanding that we must work together—with imperfect people. Things become workable and relationships become productive when we get the stars out of our eyes, put our shoulders to work, and push on toward our goals. But, to be effective, goals must have four characteristics. They must be attainable, stretching, worthwhile, and understandable for commitment to remain. Goals that stretch you—call for more from you—cause you to grow, as long as you see them as reasonably attainable for you.

Setting Your Goals

Now that you have examined these seven attitudes, you are ready to apply them to yourself. Draw three barometers like the one on page 28 and label them CAREER, RELATIONSHIP, and PERSONAL. (You can further define the last one for yourself.) Ask yourself, *Which attitude describes me best right now?* For each of the three curves, what attitude have I had during the last twelve months? Then check your responses on each curve.

Discuss your answers with someone who knows you and will disagree with you if he or she feels differently from you about your attitudes. This will give you a greater appreciation of reality. Next, draw an arrow on each attitude curve to the attitude you want.

There are many shapes to your career, marriage, or personal attitude over time. With long years of experience, your curve can look like Illustration 2.

Illustration 2

With extended resignation or apathy, your curve can look like Illustration 3.

Illustration 3

For some, the curve will look like Illustration 4.

Illustration 4

Any major change in life such as a new job, a physical move, or marriage can set your attitude curve back to attitude number one, idealistic.

Now think of the impact of your attitude on others in your organization or your family. Your attitude will affect others. It will influence your ability to communicate with them. And that will change your future. Your attitude will not only make or break you, it may make or break others around you!

Making a Change

What can you do about your attitude? First, think about it. Become aware of the three underlying attitude forces or drives: *fear, forgiveness,* and *enthusiasm.* Fear often causes you to become defiant, including your fear of losing status, security, or love. When you face your fears bravely, especially your unnamed fears, you are on your way toward a new attitude, and you need never fall into resignation. Whenever you begin to feel in doubt about a new job or another significant change in your life, take a sheet of paper and write down all your reasons for feeling apprehensive. This alone can reduce your apprehension and clear your head, because the fears you look at in a straightforward way become easier to deal with than those that remain hidden.

When you become defiant, you are usually fearful of something. This can cause you to use one of the tools of covert fear or defiance: vindictiveness. For example, you might say to yourself: *He's not getting another ounce of effort out of me. I'll do exactly what he says and nothing more.*

Vindictiveness is the opposite of forgiveness, and forgiveness is exactly what can change an attitude. Forgiveness is positive and it has a certain synergy. When you give it, you get it.

The third driving force is enthusiasm. Real enthusiasm can't be painted on, because it is an inner force. You can't fake it for long. If you've got it, you can show it. But if you haven't got it, you can get it! And when you really get enthusiasm, not only do you become ignited, but you ignite the people around you. Often, the key to ignition is doing something constructively different.

What's the Alternative?

The alternative to this kind of positive change can be the loss of the desire to change—a step away from resignation. These strong words of warning contain the antidote: *"If you don't change your attitude, your attitude will change you."*

The seven attitudes described here apply not only to individuals, but to organizations as well. When management doesn't provide for individual and organizational vitality—doesn't allow individuals to push out the walls of their jobs, for instance—*the organization itself can drop into the same attitude curve.*

With this in mind, we are ready to explore further answers to the question, "What causes attitude changes in individuals—and in organizations?"

3

Bringing Your Attitudes Under Control

Beware of no man more than of yourself; we carry our worst enemies within us.

—CHARLES SPURGEON

Behind the economic bankruptcy of every organization and the vitality bankruptcy of every individual lies an attitude change that no one noticed or someone wrote off as unimportant.

All attitude changes *are* important, because they signal coming commitment or resignation, coming success or doom. They are so important to an individual and an organization and *individuals and organizations are so important to each other* that all managers and all leaders of every kind need to understand these ten "laws" about attitudes.

Ten Laws About Attitudes

1. There is nothing uncommon or mysterious about an attitude. Everyone has attitudes, and everyone can learn how to deal with them.
2. Anyone can create an attitude in himself or herself.
3. Anyone can prevent or change his or her attitude.
4. Whenever two or more people are involved, the attitudes of one ultimately will affect the other. The attitudes of both eventually will affect the organization.
5. New attitudes and changes in old attitudes are a product of a gap between:
   Expectations—what you expected in the past.
   Reality—what you find happening now.
   Desire—what you really want to happen in the future.
6. The size of the gap and the intensity of your desire to change the gap will determine both your specific attitude right now and the speed with which your attitude changes.
7. Your attitude affects both your leadership ability as an individual and the leadership position of your organization, whether it is an athletic team, business, church, government, or your family.
8. Your attitude changes are ultimately noticeable by the general public.
9. Knowledge about your attitudes is not the privileged domain of specialists, but your own responsibility and privilege.
10. Because your attitudes are invisibly created within, often long before anyone can see the results on the outside, you can discern your attitudes in yourself and similar attitudes in others, long before they result in actions.

How You Can Discern Your Attitudes

In chapter one, we explored the notion that there is nothing magic or uncommon about leadership. Just as we need not complicate leadership, neither should we complicate attitudes—or their cause—or how you discern them.

You can discern attitudes by asking three straightforward questions:

1. What did you expect?
2. What is really happening now that is different from your expectations?
3. What do you really want to happen, now that you have determined what is really happening?

Anyone can ask these questions of himself or herself and of others, in order to find the beginnings of attitude change. As long as you listen carefully without prejudging and draw your conclusions with respect for the individual, attitude discernment has nothing mysterious about it.

Let's revisit Ralph Kennedy, the man who attended IBM's Sands Point school and changed his mind—really his attitude—about his career. We'll talk with him now to determine what caused his attitude change.

"Ralph, what were your expectations when you went to Sands Point?"

"I had planned to work as an instructor at an education facility until retirement."

"Why?"

"I thought that was the most enjoyable and comfortable way to finish my career. I liked my job, and I thought I would be content in it."

"But after you left the Sands Point school, you negotiated a different job and ended in the White House. Was something happening that was different from your expectations?"

"Yes. Down underneath, when I really thought about it, I wanted something more. I knew I wouldn't be happy to keep doing what I was doing."

"What did you really want?"

"I wanted to get back into sales again. I didn't dream I could get the White House job. But my manager listened to me, and I got the job."

"How old were you then, Ralph?"

"Fifty-one."

"Thinking of the seven attitudes discussed at Sands Point, Ralph, tell us how you related to them."

"I had dipped in my attitude. I might have been frustrated or even resigned, but I pulled back up, and now I'm committed."

This conversation is not an idle supposition. I interviewed Ralph Kennedy while making a videotape on the impact of the professional leadership program he had attended, and he related the reactions you have just read. Ralph explained how he had reviewed his past expectations, looked at his current observations about where he really stood, and discovered his desire for something more.

Bridging the Expectation Gap

As I have talked with many career people over the years, with men and women alike, I have discovered the powerful impact of defining gaps between past expectations, present perception of reality, and what people really want in the future. When these gaps are clearly seen, I have found that attitudes tend to change, as long as there is an emphasis on doing something about them. When people decide to do something different, their behavior changes, and powerful new achievements occur.

Ralph Kennedy could have stayed in the same place in his career, but he'd have missed a new level of achievement, and his management would have lost a key contribution from Ralph. The result would have been less overall productivity. *Because his attitude changed,* Ralph achieved more for himself and for his organization. This is the key to the beginning of vitality and leadership.

The key to revitalization lies not, as many suspect, in the behavioral aspects of human activity. As important as behavior may seem, it only evidences—or shows the results of—something powerful already going on in an individual's life. You might say behaviorists study what people do *after something else has already caused it.* By the time they study the behavior, something has already influenced the person's life. We must go back one important step, to examine the beginnings or the spark of vitality itself.

What creates the spark of vitality? How do you ignite it?

New vitality, new attitudes, new leadership start with straightforward questions that cause awareness—the fifth attitude. When you feel challenged to answer the gap questions we have been discussing, you look for personal gaps and ways to close them. Then things start to happen. New vitality begins as you move from awareness to decisiveness to commitment. It can happen in a number of ways. In a diagram, the expectation gap looks like Illustration 5.

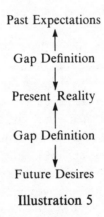

Past Expectations

↑

Gap Definition

↓

Present Reality

↑

Gap Definition

↓

Future Desires

Illustration 5

Let's experiment. For a few moments suppose that you have a gap between your past expectations and your present circumstances. This will help you see that you can make several changes to close the gaps for yourself. But that depends on the *level* of your expectations, your present *feelings* about them, and the *strength* of your desires. First, a few questions: What were your past expectations about your organization, career, job, or family? Pick one of these areas of your personal interest and think about your past expectations. Does the present match them? What do you really want to happen now?

Let's suppose you had high expectations, you have a satisfying feeling about them now, and you have a desire to continue on your present path. Now you are reaching for yet higher expectations, deeper satisfactions, and you have the desire to see your hopes achieved. For such an individual, attitudes are generally positive, life is good and motivation is normal.

But suppose you had high expectations and few of them worked out. You really feel dissatisfied with this. But your desire to try again remains so strong that you are ready to put all your energy to work to make things happen the way you expected. If that is so, you have moved from awareness to decisiveness and may well be knocking on the door of commitment.

You could also go a third way: high expectations, low results, discouragement.

Actually, in several ways these three factors—past expectations, present reality, and future desires—can work together to cause different results or behavior. But suppose for a moment that you had low expectations and have achieved average success—you haven't failed and you haven't turned your world upside down. Suppose also that you feel content to let things remain as they are, and you have little desire for new achievement. Such a person will not change the organization in the future, unless desire changes—unless a spark occurs. There is nothing wrong or right about this person and no need to judge. If you or someone you know has reached this place in life, you will discover many others there, too. Such individuals maintain the much needed functions that every organization has, and should be left alone. But some people have given up. They are the uncoiled springs in life. Still others have burned out.

Is there a way to come back from burnout? Is there a way to put new spring into an uncoiled spring? We'll look at some people who have turned their wipeouts into successes and at the techniques you can use to make your career more profitable—whatever it is!

4

Getting
a New
Perspective
on Where
You Are

*When the fight begins within himself, a man's worth
something.*

—ROBERT BROWNING

When thirteen men from DuPont arrived at Eagle
Lodge, a few miles from Valley Forge, Pennsylvania, on
a drizzly Sunday evening in May, they had little idea of
what lay ahead for them. They knew they were carefully
selected professional leaders, but like the colonial troops
at Valley Forge, they didn't know what they were to do.

These thirteen had contributed to the marketing
achievements of a world-famous business giant that had
helped shape America's success since the early years of

41

the nation. From gunpowder, in the 1800s, through nylon, in the Second World War, and huge plasticlike cables that hold our ocean-top oil-drilling platforms to the ocean floor, the DuPont Corporation had become a powerful innovator of American business vitality. This same innovative spirit and interest in the employees paved the way for the New Perspectives experiment at DuPont.

Now, as I faced these thirteen men, ranging in age from their mid-fifties to the mid-thirties, I remember thinking that they likely had deep motivations and hopes in common with other men and women I had taught in American business. So I shared some startling statements about modern career life. I had watched reactions of thousands of middle-level managers in American Management Association programs and other organizations across America, so I felt a kinship with these men even before I saw their responses. No real difference exists in the attitudes, hopes, and expectations of experienced managers and employees across American business.

"Listen to these powerful statements from others like you," I told the group. "Then think of your own expectations." I began reading aloud some of the statements of experienced employees that I had used over the years.

Attitude Statements of Some Experienced Employees

- "I was on a fast track once. Now I'm on a railroad siding, and I don't know where I'm heading."
- "On his deathbed nobody ever says he wished he'd spent more time in his business."
- "This company is like a velvet coffin. You lose your life, but you feel so secure."

As I read a series of such statements, I felt by their reactions that these thirteen men had past expectations and experiences similar to those of thousands of employees across America. I read the statements not to raise concerns, but to remove a protective layer many employees develop, which covers over and impedes their professional vitality and leadership. Often employees have this layer without knowing it. The idea is to find the real spark of leadership beneath the veneer of protectionism. All employees experience this sometime in their work life, and it literally saps their energy. For this reason many long-service employees and managers are seen as crusty, skeptical people who need to be overmanaged, rather than as lifelong professionals who create solutions at work, without the need for much direction.

Beneath the layer of protection lies a universal desire to become a vital, creative, innovative professional. The renewal of this vitality starts with an honest look at self as well as the organization. With that calculated risk, the DuPont New Perspectives School started, and it paid off. I had asked management if they would appear on Tuesday to answer questions and sample the participants' reactions, then appear again on Friday for a further sampling. I promised management a significant change in every person by Friday. In five days, these thirteen men—already handpicked people with solid skills—became more confident, more prepared to return to their jobs with a commitment to take total responsibility as professional leaders, rather than be reactionaries. DuPont's interest in its valuable long-service employees had paid off. Here's how.

On Monday, they got rid of their attitude layer and looked at their own ability to listen effectively on the job. On Tuesday, they examined their individual styles of working with people and went to work on three professional leadership issues, using their newfound skill in listening and utilizing people with differing work styles. By Wednesday, they learned that each day was a totally new perspective. They considered the idea that each person had not only the ability, but the responsibility to manage himself. After their first two and a half days, the thirteen men examined their physical teamwork, then returned to examine their attitudes on the job. Each day involved a new discovery for them as they were constantly challenged to do something different with each new day and to become catalysts for the others as the week went on. On Thursday, they learned to critically reexamine everything they had been taught and to begin to reset their own career plans while working on the organization issues they were assigned to resolve. This combined focus on individual and organizational vitality was designed to benefit both themselves and DuPont. From the start of the week each person knew he had to make group recommendations, as well as individual *leadership commitments* in front of the entire group. To get ready, each worked voluntarily, far into the night on Thursday.

On Friday morning, tired but determined, every one of these sophisticated long-service professionals stood up and reported his personal plan for both professional and personal leadership, and each did it in a way that made an unforgettable impact on the others. It is difficult to describe that meeting, or the week, in sufficient detail, but the results will give some feeling for the impact that thirteen men can make in their jobs and in their organizations. When management met with the graduates on Friday, they were struck by the change that had occurred. As a result, management approved a special two-day follow-up reunion to determine whether the change would persist.

Five months later, a two-day class was held, and twelve of the thirteen met again at Eagle Lodge.

Revitalization at Work

In October of that year, each graduate reported his experience as a professional leader. Their individual experiences varied, but they exhibited an immediate cohesiveness as a group of professional leaders. Before me I saw a changed group of people—a group who could make comments like these:

- "I'm in an aeronautics marketing area, and I proposed that DuPont pay for a pilot's license, so I could get more understanding, and they did it! Now I'm titled a group leader. I

44

don't have people responsibility, but I have leadership responsibility. I've even been writing some marketing articles."

- "On the job I've reached up and grabbed for more! It's like military experience: If you take the noncommissioned officers out, the organization would fall on its rear. We run this corporation. If we left or if we all caught the blue flu, the business would come to a screeching halt. I'm learning how to say, 'This is *my* place!' People are coming to *me* for advice as a result of this program."
- "I'm in a new job with a new product in a new geographic area and a new home. Having been here before, I will be better in this new job—more confident in me."
- "On the job, I've taken on a major new account and given up nothing. Now I know that I can expand my job. Off the job, my golf handicap dropped two points. I've begun to look at all my priorities. I realize now that I've got to get away with my wife more often."
- "I decided I was going to run my job as a consultant. Now I'm asking some questions I learned here: Who is important and what is important—and that is giving me more confidence."
- "Now I have the ability to really communicate with the graduates. I came out of the school like a skyrocket."
- "I said I'd really try my new job. I sold some new PC pilots in my department. Now that a colleague is retiring I plan to make an impact on the selection of a replacement. I met with the top marketing staff with a report on this school—a meeting that couldn't have happened before."
- "What was said at our follow-up meeting was said in the right way. We are seen as a resource!"
- "The team leader concept is being tried. I have more confidence, more freedom at work."
- ". . . I vowed to be less reactive and more pro-active. I vowed to be heard for my innovative ideas."
- "I was puzzled about my selection for New Perspectives, but I

came away knowing I was a professional. It was a quiet confidence, but my secretary thought I was a wild man because of all the extra work I did. I've taken two new accounts and a new employee. I'm acknowledged even more now. I'm the lead professional. Now I've been offered a tremendous job with a customer. If I accept I will be heading a division in the new company, and I'll be an officer. Would I have taken the job before? Maybe. But now I *know* I can handle it."

- "Things have gone awfully well for me. I said I would push out the boundaries of my job and reach out to people."

One of the graduates said in a letter to his management:

Now, What Is Happening? Another way to ask this question is, what does DuPont get back for the money invested in this course? Perhaps the best way to answer this is to say that DuPont gets back a more self-motivated group of employees— more willing to push out the real and perceived boundaries of our jobs—and more willing to help and reinforce each other. I have certainly found this to be true, and observed the same in others. "Professional leadership" is the course motto, and I think we have begun to think of ourselves that way. We have all begun to redefine our personal goals, based on greater appreciation of our individual strengths and weaknesses. We now clearly understand how DuPont views our potential—but not all of us may be willing to accept this.

Unfortunately, there is a tremendous amount of talent lying fallow. This is largely due to frustration, lack of motivation, and job placement. Now we can overcome the first two by ourselves and understand that we can impact the third. Once again, this was the most important experience of my career—and it's staying with me! Back to work now—I've got an interesting new job to learn!

As this letter implies, changing and revitalizing an organization means carefully selecting people with significant talents, who can become vitality catalysts for the good of the organization as well as for each other and themselves. But once professional leaders return to work, how do they go about the task of becoming vitality catalysts? What happens if management doesn't *want* professional leaders who push out the walls of their jobs? Clearly there is risk here, if the organization isn't ready. But tremendous payoffs accrue to the organization willing to invest in professional leadership at all levels. First, we will look at ways to encourage professional leaders, including all levels of managers, to act as "vitality catalysts" in your organization. Here are ten guidelines adapted from professional leader Don Cochrane's list that will start individual revitalization for everyone who wants to be a professional leader.

Ten Guidelines for Professional Leaders and Managers

1. Understand yourself in terms of your background, beliefs, experiences, current role, and future plans.
2. Understand the environment in which you're operating as broadly as possible. Seek new ways to experience your world's activities by setting high objectives for yourself.
3. Develop a perspective of the differences between the managerial and nonmanagerial responsibilities of your business, organization, and department.
4. Learn to articulate meaningful opinions on issues as they arise, based on your understanding of yourself, the business, the environment, and the facts of the situation.
5. Look for the underlying issues that no one is addressing but that ought to be addressed. Learn to define them with clarity and to present them with a constructive attitude.
6. Identify and address long-known or newly discovered negative influences on the qualitative progress of individuals or the business unit.
7. Be real—open, honest, and self-critical—in all endeavors. Care-

fully break down barriers to understanding. Don't overlook the presence and the value of emotion in every situation.

8. Step back and look at your organization, your manager, and your total enterprise as though you are a consultant who is paid to think strategically. Take care to prepare recommendations you can implement now.

9. Approach your organization as a responsible salesman. Show people what's in your idea that will help and why it should be done.

10. Sit in your chief executive's chair and learn to ask the following penetrating questions about your own recommendations! These will add depth and responsibility to your work.

If I were the chief executive officer:

- Could I afford to do this?
- Could I afford not to do it?
- How will it help my organization right now?
- How will it help my organization in the next few years?

The results of a vitality-catalyst effort can make your organization outdistance your competition—or, without the proper preparation, it could tear up a few established relationships within your own organization. Again, no organization should decide to initiate a vitality-catalyst effort without a willingness to risk. But then, all decisions involve risk, otherwise no change occurs. With all that considered, there is a way to overcome the risks by preparing the managers of renewed professional leaders.

Once again, the DuPont Corporation has shown its long history of trying out creative new ways to be innovative and to help its employees remain vital. We will not forget the question raised a few moments ago: What happens if management in your organization doesn't want professional leaders who push out the walls of their jobs? But first, consider what can happen if you *don't* allow it. You have seen the seven attitudes that can make or break you and your organization. They apply to employees, managers, and people in general, just as they did to the New Perspectives graduates at IBM and DuPont. Now let's see how you can turn your attitudes to new motivation, even beyond the motivation of your past.

5

What Really Motivates You?

Remember that what pulls the strings is the force hidden within; there lies the power to persuade, there the life—there, if one must speak out, the real man.

—MARCUS AURELIUS

What motivates business America? How can organizations motivate people throughout their entire careers? To answer complex questions we need to get back to the basics.

For years Abraham Maslow's hierarchy of needs and Frederick Herzberg's ideas on motivation were dominant forces in American business. These two men thought much alike, and they made a positive impact on American management. But now we need to take a fresh look at what motivates you.

Maslow identified five developmental levels of need that a person can have satisfied. Each builds upon the last, and one must be fulfilled before the next level can be reached. They form a triangle, as shown in Illustration 6.

Maslow's Hierarchy

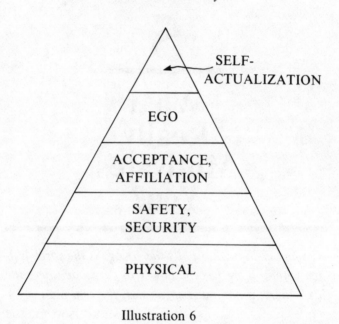

Illustration 6

Maslow described self-actualization as the ultimate motivation, though he modified this toward the end of his life, and Herzberg emphasized work itself as a motivator. Both brought their Jewish heritage of individualism to work and drew on it in writing about motivation. Much they said proved helpful, but they focused heavily on self-interest.

For a moment think beyond self-interest. What happens after people establish themselves in their careers and find self-actualization? Is self-interest the ultimate source of our motivation? History shows that people through the centuries were motivated not only by self-interest, but by causes, personal mission, discovery, service, beliefs, and creativity itself.

We won't discount the things that Maslow, Herzberg, and others have said. We will go on from there, because there is more to the story of motivation.

In thirty years of business experience, teaching, counseling, and building management programs on local, national, and international levels, I have found that people reach a point in life when self-interest isn't enough. Not nearly enough.

In one year of working as program manager for IBM's Community Executive Program, my colleagues and I taught hundreds of nonprofit executives from the Red Cross, Boy Scouts, Girl Scouts, Heart Association, YMCA, YWCA, United Way, NAACP, and scores of other organizations, representing Latin, Asian, African, and American cultures, as well as Jewish and Christian heritages. Most of the executives were drawn into America's $40 billion plus nonprofit sector by a sense of service as well as self. They were looking for a way to help, not just to be helped. They were looking for a worthwhile cause.

Religious motivations have endured, even though impacted by self-serving motives. America was explored not only by self-interested people, but by purpose-motivated Christians and Jews as well. Why do people give up possessions, birthrights, family life, citizenship, personal freedom, even life itself for causes beyond themselves? Both history and current social action give us evidence of motivation that includes but goes beyond self-interest.

Four Commitment Motivations

I have found that people want to fulfill four purpose or commitment motivations at some time in their lives. Mature people need:

- to serve
- to believe

- to recognize
- to act decisively and creatively

When individuals practice all four motivations at work or at home, they learn how to become committed. Such people produce—responsibly, reliably, enthusiastically—over a lifetime. Organizations as well as individuals need commitment motivation. Because America's employees are growing older, living longer, staying in their jobs and looking for purpose fulfillment—or just hanging around—motivation has become a much more critical factor in today's business world.

What will America do with an aging work force if it becomes purpose motivated? With more older workers remaining longer and looking for something more worthwhile, organizations must find new ways to utilize the people who won't retire and the organization can't (and shouldn't) fire. The answer: retain the best self-interest motivation and add the best commitment motivation you can discover. Commitment, purpose, leadership, and vitality are equally as important as security, safety, and self-actualization. Anyone can have them all, to some degree. Everyone needs them all. In the long run, organizations cannot survive without paying attention to commitment motivation as well as self-service motivation.

Commitment motivation includes beliefs and principles that people can follow. An organization needs a written statement of purpose or belief. The undergirding cultural strength of IBM's worldwide management development program emphasizes a balance of three basic beliefs:

- respect for the individual
- excellence in everything that is done
- the best possible service to the customer

These three compelling beliefs all deal with principles of personal and business relationship. The commitment of IBM's leadership to these beliefs is poured into the lifeblood of the company and shows up in often repeated statements: "We will change everything we need to change, but we won't change our basic beliefs." Such commitment holds organizations on course over the years. Beliefs such as these mesh with the four commitment needs of people and apply to both nonprofit and profit organizations. Look again at the motivations of mature people.

- to serve completely
- to believe wholeheartedly
- to recognize immediately
- to act decisively and creatively

To Serve Completely

Beyond self-interest, people want to experience complete service and wholehearted belief. I believe that each of these four motivations applies equally to organizations as well as to individuals in them. Think of some of the best organizations you know. They try to serve completely, whether they are elegant restaurants or fast-food chains. People respect complete service. They seek it, pay for it, and demand it.

To Believe Wholeheartedly

The best organizations believe wholeheartedly in their mission, products, services, and principles of operation. Unless the people within can trust the organization to follow solid principles, the organization faces the constant danger of obsolescence.

To Recognize Immediately

The best organizations have learned to recognize good performance immediately, how to foster it, how to recognize swiftly when things aren't going well.

To Act Decisively and Creatively

The best organizations have learned how to act decisively and creatively to meet the changing needs of their customers and employees. They know that meeting one set of needs alone will not suffice in the future, and they look to the requirements ahead.

What Does It Take to Motivate?

The triangular look of Maslow's needs hierarchy really is only one side of a three-sided pyramid. Illustration 7 reveals another side. The third will be revealed in chapter 19.

Two Sides of Motivation

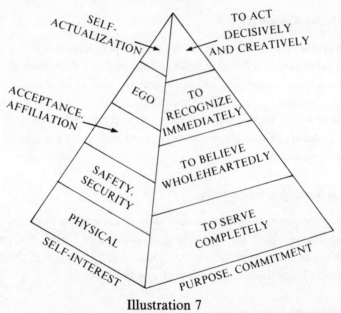

Illustration 7

Once you are willing to look at more than one side of a person's motivation, you can begin to deal with the whole person in a practical way. That does not mean you need to become entangled with deep issues of philosophy or psychology. When you consider what motivates people, you usually are aiming for results that help your organization. With a wink in his eye, one man defined motivation as "getting people to do what you want them to do." But that's not motivation, it's manipulation.

What *does* it take to motivate people? Dr. John Geier spent his career looking into this question. He became president of Performax, a highly successful Minneapolis-based firm that produced a number of helpful motivation instruments. John Geier says, "You can't motivate people, because people are motivated already. They will do things, but for their own reasons."

The key in dealing with people is not to become over-involved in why people do things in general, but to ask specific people straightforward questions, so you can understand what *this* person really feels motivated to do. There is no need to complicate motivation, just as there is no need to complicate leadership or attitudes.

Dr. John Hinrichs, president of Management Decision Systems, author of *Practical Management for Productivity,* and a fellow of the American Psychological Association, simplifies motivation for us when he says, "There hasn't been much new in the field of behavioral discovery [not attitudinal discovery] over the last twenty years. There are only a few usable verities that have come from behavioral research in that time." Hinrichs adds, "These are practical insights you can use in your organization and your own career."

Five Usable Verities From Behavioral Experience

1. The best predictor of future performance is past performance.
2. Setting difficult but attainable performance goals and providing regular feedback enhances motivation and performance.
3. Rewarding performance equitably enhances job satisfaction.
4. Groups can produce synergistically—can produce more than the individuals can separately—when goals are shared and developed together.

5. Many jobs can be redesigned to enhance their motivational effectiveness.

These are solid clues to get maximum short-term productivity using behavioral principles. They have worked for thousands of organizations in America, and you can continue to reap a harvest of productivity by using them. But you must remember one essential thing: The behavioral approach requires somebody around to set goals. What would happen if you could tap a person's commitment motivation *and* his self-interest motivation so that you use long-term motivation and short-term motivation *at the same time?* You could reap the benefits of both behavioral and attitudinal concepts and require less managerial time.

If an organization or an individual gets stalled on the tracks, as most people do sometime in their careers, you can tap the existing motivation of the individual, *whatever it is.* You can get an organization moving again by getting key people moving again. You don't need to be a specialist or a psychologist to do it. Combine the things you have learned about self-interest motivation with commitment motivation—attitude and vitality with leadership. You can revitalize people, focus their vision, give them a purpose, use their individual motivation, produce professional leaders, and place your organization in a leadership position. But before you start, you will need to thoroughly understand six subtle yet important clues behind what you have been reading. These will help you get where you want to go faster.

Six Motivation Clues

1. Select experienced people who have already proven their performance ability. (The best predictor of future performance is past performance.)
2. Let individuals know you care. Listen to them without prejudging. (Remove the protective layer that hides the vitality spark.)

3. Ask straightforward questions of each individual about past expectations, present perceptions, and future desires. (There's no need to guess at attitudes or motivations or to make things complicated. Ask questions.)

4. Show the people the real issues, goals, and needs of your organization. Give them a cause, a purpose bigger than themselves. (History shows that people respond to causes and have a need to be committed to something really worthwhile.)

5. Challenge individuals to work together to create strategic solutions. (When goals are shared and developed together, groups can produce more than individuals can separately.)

6. Give individuals a second chance to be professional leaders. Urge them to do something constructively different as a way to be a leader. (Leadership is not an uncommon trait.)

Does all of this sound complicated? The reality is that none of this is as difficult as many believe. Can something be done about motivation in your organization? Are you interested in doing something about it? If so, you may already be a professional leader inside. You can begin to bring your ability out into the open!

Step by step we are laying out the road map for changing business America. It starts with your organization, beginning with individuals like you. You will find the next step in chapter 6: "Pushing Out the Walls of Your Professional Life." That's where you will find how jobs, perhaps including yours, can be redesigned to enhance motivational effectiveness.

6

Pushing Out the Walls of Your Professional Life

Of course we all have our limits, but how can you possibly find your boundaries unless you explore as far and as wide as you possibly can? I would rather fail in an attempt at something new and uncharted than safely succeed in a repeat of something I have done.
—A. E. HOTCHNER

How many times have you heard someone say, "I'm sick of this job. It doesn't offer me anything anymore." Often you have watched the person wait around for months, even years, slipping into frustration, defiance, and resignation, but doing nothing constructive about the job.

But what if that person tries something constructive? Sometimes a manager perceives the problem quite differently and he or she becomes the problem. "If Charlie gets too many new ideas he'll start asking questions. He'll get unhappy and start crowding me for something new. I don't have any other openings right now and this work's got to be done."

This is where new beginnings of motivation, professional leadership, and productivity can die while they are yet being born.

Managers with this kind of attitude feel about jobs the way an old mechanic feels about working on cars. "If it ain't broke, don't fix it." That kind of wisdom works with many things, but it doesn't work with motivation, because it's harder to tell whether something is not working within people, where motivation dwells. People lose their vitality *inside* long before others find out—usually, long before the person himself faces up to it.

Whether you are a manager or a professional, you can find new purpose in the responsibility you have right now by pushing out the walls of your job and redefining the purpose. Doing this will give you new perspective, let you see the real dimensions of your work as you've never seen them before, and allow you to do the job differently, for the good of your organization, your own well-being, and your professional growth for the future.

You should never go to another job until you have pushed out the walls of the job you have right now. This means that your assignment is not complete until you have tackled it with the idea that you can leave it more explored, understood and developed than it was when you took it. That way, you will get more from it while you give more to it. A mental attitude that focuses on the buried treasure in every job heals people of the blindness they develop when they accept work without knowing its purpose. Whether you have been in your job for three days, three months, three years or thirteen years, it's time to take another look at what the organization really needs to accomplish while you look at what *you* are actually accomplishing. We're not talking about changing the job just for the sake of change. That would disrupt the good things going on. The idea is to look at your work differently.

When you bought your house or rented your apartment, you tried to notice everything about your new place. You inspected the walls for quality, appearance, and feel. In effect, you asked yourself several questions, *Will this serve the purpose? Can I be comfortable? Is there anything I'm going to need to change here?* Your inquiring attitude brought discernment to your decision. In the same way, a constructive, questioning attitude at work opens the way for new discovery and new opportunity for motivation right where you are.

Questions are your powerful tools to locate and explore the walls of your job, so you can reconstruct it as it should be. Good questions are the shovels that dig up the buried treasure in your job. Questions are the way you define and clarify your own expectations, and the expectations of your management. In the same way that you as an employee must push out the walls of your job, you as a manager can *allow* your employees to do this, and reap the benefits of a motivated work force. If you are in a position of management, your attitude can be "If it's not running smoothly, it'll break!"

Often, busy managers haven't thought about what they really want done when a new person comes aboard. Managers at all levels need to go beyond the point of getting a replacement or someone new to do the work at hand. A manager as well as a person assuming the responsibility itself must ask questions at the *beginning* of every job change. Putting questions to work before you put people to work will likely change the job itself, and the motivating power of the assignment. This is your opportunity to put purpose motivation to work for you.

Most jobs look as if they started with a set of walls, or responsibilities, when they should start with the purpose. The walls of a room merely exist to carry out the purpose of the room, and that's the way a job should be. You can change the walls of your job by putting the purpose or the desired end result *first*. Here is a list of questions that will help you, whether you are a professional desiring to find the real purpose of your task, or whether you are a manager deciding what you really need to accomplish.

Redefining the Boundaries of the Job

1. What is the mission or purpose of the organization I work in?
2. What is the purpose or end result of *this* job in the organization?
3. What am I trying to create?
4. What problems am I trying to resolve?
5. What specific steps are there in this job as it now exists?
6. What new steps are needed?
7. What steps should be removed?
8. How will I know when this job is done well?
9. What *self-interest* motivation is there in this assignment?
10. What *purpose* motivation is there in this job?

These ten questions can help you see not only what the job is, but what it should be—and how it can become more productive.

I have made a remarkable personal discovery over the years. Most jobs can be changed in some way, often in an easier way than it seemed, to make the work more valuable to the organization and more motivating to me. Further, when I have changed my jobs over the years—redefined them and showed the way I felt they should be done—I automatically created more room to do them in. Then management became more inclined to leave me to do the work.

That is the way to get new vitality in your work. Take a look at the responsibility you hold right now. Somebody decided what the job should be two or perhaps even twenty years ago. In effect, the walls of your job were erected to solve a two-year or a twenty-year-old problem. Whether you are an executive with people under you or a professional with people over you, your job is *yours*, however old it is. It is your opportunity and your responsibility to personally resist the idea that people should fit into job descriptions, as long as you can constructively replace that idea with this new one: *People should fit into job purpose, not into job description.* Job description—

what the work looks like—will flow out of the job purpose, and become a more vital addition to the organization than a job that starts with a description alone. Job purposes seldom flow out of descriptions. Even if your old job description is still appropriate for today's job, you can improve it when you rebuild it on today's purpose or foundation of the job.

What you need to see in the organization around you is an attitude that makes people approach their tasks with a new perspective that catches the system by surprise. The way to do that is to create a climate where everyone looks at his or her job as an architectural consultant. Here's how to get started.

Most jobs have a roof over them that needs to be lifted off, and the walls need to be removed, exposing the foundation. Often the foundation needs to be examined to see if it can carry more weight. Finally, a job needs to be examined to see if the mission or the title is clear. Does anyone else have ownership of this work? Is there a duplicate claim to the ownership of *this* job?

> *When people see the purpose of their work, they will have purpose motivation. When people see the description of the job, they will have self-interest motivation. When people see the mission or the title of their responsibility, they will develop personal identification and ownership of it.*

Let's look more closely at work in this new way. Most jobs can be divided into four "rooms," or sections, which call for different activities. Many people work only on steps or responsibilities of their job, when they could work in job "rooms" that allow new perspective, space, and growth. Working in rooms rather than on tasks can keep people productive and motivated for years, and the value of their work and their value as individuals will increase measurably if they work in more than one job room. The rooms of a job look like Illustration 8.

The Four Rooms or Sections of a Job

I Relationship Responsibilities	II Analytical- Judgmental Responsibilities
IV Managerial- Administrative Responsibilities	III Creative- Innovative Responsibilities

Illustration 8

Illustration 9 shows how a job really looks with the purpose, rooms (or sections), and mission well defined.

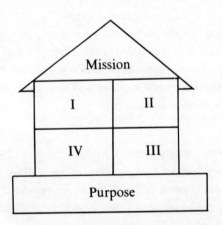

Illustration 9

To really become more vital and productive, you can find ways to push out the walls of your job. First, use the ten questions you already read to fully define the purpose of your job. Then, decide which is your strongest room, or area, then your next strongest, your third strongest, and finally your least strong.

Next, write three to five specific responsibilities that fit into each room. If you find it hard to list any responsibilities in one room, you have just discovered an area of your assignment that may need major reconstruction.

If you can become effective in three out of the four rooms of your job—or even better, all four rooms—you will be more valuable to your organization and yourself.

Often organizations neglect to see that every job that exists has four separate rooms or areas that can be more fully occupied. When an employee expands into another room or area of his or her responsibility, or pushes out the walls of all four rooms, he will be better able to define the purpose of the job and will become more motivated and more productive in the same job. Following this approach, you will find the responsibility becomes bigger and makes more impact on the organization. This is good for everyone, as long as no one pushes out the walls so far that the roof falls in.

Sometimes, a person pushes out the walls of a job so much that he can't handle it. At this point management must decide whether the activities fit the mission of the job and the organization. If they do, yet the job has become too big, some of the less important responsibilities must be cut out or additional people must occupy the rooms and do the work.

This job-room approach is not an idle idea. I've done this with my own assignments for many years. Further, I installed a job-room description program for an insurance company. It provided a way for people to see what their jobs really were, and what they could be.

New vitality, motivation, purpose and productivity start at the individual level. What individuals need is a new perspective of their personal role, and they need to know how to push out the walls of their professional life. The next chapter, "Occupying Your Expanded Job," will show you how to make any job not just a place to work, but a place to explore, to grow in and to recreate vitality.

7

Occupying Your Expanded Job

I am convinced that one of the biggest factors in success is the courage to undertake something.

—JAMES A. WORSHAM

Once you have decided that your job can become something more, that it has at least four rooms rather than a set of job tasks, you have the beginnings of new vitality at work, without changing managers or jobs. Here's how you can set about furnishing the rooms in your job.

Make a Physical Change

First, as you start the process of fully developing your job potential look for some tangible way to let others know that you are bringing a new perspective. Even if

69

you have been in the job for a while, you can change the furniture, move the desk, hang a picture, do something different with your physical environment. Also let your changes be a statement to yourself that you will approach your job differently.

I found a surprising difference in the reactions of people around me and an impact on my own approach when I moved my desk from the middle of my office to a wall. It opened up the floor space and allowed me to greet visitors without sitting behind the desk. A corner of my office became the area for desk work and another became the area for discussing ideas. Whenever I could, I even moved the phone so I had to get up to answer it. I looked for physical ways to change my approach to the job so that I would bring mental vitality to it.

Your office or work area need not be large, but it does need to be unique in some way, as a visible reminder that you are occupying the space in a different way, with a new attitude.

Make a Mental Change

Next, create a new visual look in your job responsibilities, just as you created a new look in your office or work area. You can create a new perspective of your job by rearranging your responsibilities on a piece of paper. When you do this, you will see your present job differently, and in time others will notice, just as they noticed your changed work area. Surprisingly this works at all levels, from the chief executive officer down to the newest employee. Here's how a trainer did it: Illustration 10 shows his new approach when he viewed his job as having four sections, or rooms, of responsibilities, rather than the responsibility of instruction alone.

If these sections or rooms of the job appear unusual, keep in mind that the job of a trainer depends on your approach to it, more than on someone's initial statement of the responsibilities alone. When you say to yourself, *I'm going to really explore this job to see what it* should *be,* you have increased the likelihood of discovering the real job. You open the door to the potential vitality contained in the job, and you open the door to greater contribution to your organization.

Four Rooms in a Trainer's Job

I Instructor (Relationship)	II Planner (Analytical-Judgmental)
IV Manager (Managerial-Administrative)	III Consultant (Creative-Innovative)

Illustration 10

To make it easier to explore the trainer's job, or any job, you can use six powerful tools or questions to help you. Use these already familiar questions:

- What is the real purpose of this job?
- What relationship responsibilities are there in this job, if it is done well?
- What analytical–judgmental responsibilities are there?
- What creative–innovative responsibilities are there?
- What managerial or administrative responsibilities are there?
- What is the mission or title of this job?

These six questions can lead you to think about a job from six different points of view. First, the purpose of the trainer's job: to teach employees to do something the organization needs done more efficiently and more productively.

Next, the four rooms or sections of the job: When you imagine yourself in each of the four rooms, even though you can't see them, you can begin to think more creatively and more productively about the real job that exists beyond the conventional walls of the original job description. You begin to think not only about what *is* in the job, but what *should* be in the job, *if it is done with excellence.* It's like asking, "What furniture does this job room need?" or "How should the present furniture be rearranged?" Now you are on your way toward revitalizing the job, just because you have a different approach. Anyone can look at a job from a new perspective.

When you consider a trainer's job the way we've been suggesting, you find that training doesn't involve just instructing someone in class. It includes planning the right things to instruct. It also requires consulting, because the right things to instruct come from consulting with managers who want an organization problem solved or people to perform differently. The instructor must also create the right training at the right time for the right people. Finally, real instruction begins when the class is established and the student practices the skills the instructor teaches.

The real trainer's job has a purpose or foundation, the four separate focuses (or rooms) just described and a roof or a name that describes the mission of the person occupying it. The real job is more suitably titled "organization skills developer," rather than "trainer," and the trainer saw it more clearly as he filled in the specific things that really needed to be done in each job room in Illustration 10. The rooms now contain specific skills and tasks, as shown in Chart 1.

Now, with the addition of a purpose, the furnished rooms that provide new perspective, and a clear title or mission, you can see that the original trainer job has long-term potential for personal growth and four separate skill areas or rooms to work in. Suppose you were to do something like this with your job. Even if your management doesn't see the job the same way, *you* will see ways to develop your skills and to help the organization by working in the other rooms of your job when there is an opportunity. Your vision

Job Title or Mission
Organization Skills Developer

Relationship Responsibilities
(INSTRUCTOR)

- Conducts classroom activities to meet program objectives
- Conveys and interprets information and concepts to students
- Responds flexibly to class needs
- Leads classes in learning

Analytical-Judgmental Responsibilities
(PROGRAM PLANNER)

- Defines training needs
- Sets course objectives
- Picks training methods
- Uses appropriate education programs
- Measures program effectiveness

Managerial-Administrative Responsibilities
(MANAGER)

- Develops overall program strategy
- Secures financial and physical resources
- Schedules and publicizes programs
- Enrolls students and speakers

Creative-Innovative Responsibilities
(CONSULTANT)

- Responds to requests for help from management
- Helps others to identify problems and finds solutions
- Creates new education programs
- Initiates recommendations to management

JOB PURPOSE: Determine what the organization needs done and teach employees to do it, more efficiently and productively, for the mutual benefit of the organization and the individual.

Chart 1

73

of the job in the future and your approach to the job today never will be quite the same once you have seen the potential for additional contribution and new skill growth that exists. The key to vitality in your current job is to ask questions that help you look at your skill areas as though they are empty rooms that require furnishing.

Every job has potential for growth and new learning in relationships, judgment, creativity, and managerial skills. By listing tasks that belong in each room and doing some of them, you change the job. But more than that, you change your *approach* to the job. That is what job vitality is all about. Some jobs have more room for creativity and innovation than others. Some jobs have more relationship potential than analytical potential. But all jobs have buried treasure in one or more rooms. Enter *all* the rooms, decide what tasks belong there, and start doing the tasks when you can. Just do it. That's professional leadership.

If you have no creative-innovative responsibilities, you can create some. You will receive more salary consideration, obtain more latitude, and enjoy more purpose motivation if you do something creative or innovative that no one else has done in your job. But you'll need to work the changes out with management above you, to pave the way. Otherwise you may find only reasons why something shouldn't be done. It takes only one reason why something *should* be done. In your career that reason is job vitality.

Take a look at your job, however big or small it is. Look carefully at all its rooms. Even if only one thing in one room needs doing, you will give more to the job and take more from it, if you do that one thing. If more than one thing needs doing, pick the one you like most to do, and do it. In so doing, you automatically become an innovator. It's only a matter of time before someone notices a difference. Even if that someone is you alone, you have gained added experience that you can use elsewhere. But what happens if there aren't any more rooms than those you see around you?

When I moved from upstate New York to the suburbs of Washington, D.C., I bought a house too big for my family. I had the feeling that someday my parents might need to move in with us in their retirement years. We had plenty of basement space off the recreation room, so I decided to make two additional rooms out of the empty basement space. I knew that I wasn't a builder, but I knew what a hammer was, so I picked up my hammer one day, walked up to the recreation room wall, where I thought a door ought to be, and bashed a hole in the wall. Two of my young sons, playing in the recreation room, momentarily looked stunned at my unusual act. One said in alarm, "Dad! What are you doing?" I picked up a saw and said, "This is the way you build a door, son."

I didn't really know how to build a door, but I didn't want my sons to think that. I broke out all the wallboard to make the opening look like a doorway; then I stepped through the hole, into the basement. Fortunately, the hole was between two two-by-fours. Then I went to the lumberyard and discovered something called a prehung door. I had heard about prehung doors, but now I was ready to learn about one. I bought the door—hardware, knob, and everything all in place, and carried it down to the hole in the wall. Then I knew why the lumber dealer told me to buy the shims.

With twelve common nails, I hammered the door in place between the two-by-fours. I was delighted when it stood up. Then I put my hand on the knob, opened the door, and swung it. It clicked shut, just like a real door!

Now my sons said in whispered amazement, "Dad can build a door!" I opened and shut that door five times or so, just feeling the excitement of my whole venture. Then I stepped through the door and built two complete rooms, not knowing anything about how to do it. I hung the dropped ceiling the lumber dealer sold me. It didn't look like a ceiling when it was delivered in little bundles of thin metal strips and packages of tile, but by the time I followed directions it did. Later, I laid tile on the floor, hammered sills for walls, and built two complete rooms. It took me two years, but I enjoyed it, because *I was growing while the rooms took shape.* I found that I was no longer Don Osgood. I was Don Osgood plus two completed rooms. Nobody could ever take that experience from me. It made me realize that life is often a series of uncompleted rooms, just as jobs are.

Every job I've ever held had uncompleted rooms, and I've carried my hammer along with me into each job, quietly bashing a hole in each wall and finding that rooms that don't exist are built more easily than I thought they could be.

But sometimes, people don't appreciate holes in their walls. Sometimes a manager wonders what you're doing with the wall, especially if he thinks it's *his* wall. That's why you've got to treat managers as though the walls are theirs, even if they're not. Because relationships are as important as walls, you've got to treat managers as though they were your customers, as you will see in the next chapter.

8

Convincing Your Manager

The most important single ingredient in the formula of success is knowing how to get along with people.
—THEODORE ROOSEVELT

You not only need to push out the walls of your job so you can see it more clearly, you need to be willing to change your relationships so you can see how they too can change your job—and your professional life.

Treating your manager as your customer will make all the difference in how open your manager will be to a change that you think of as constructive but he or she may think of as destructive. No one wants to change a room in a house if it will destroy the value of that house.

Your Manager as Customer

It doesn't matter who you are, how high your level in management or nonmanagement, or how secure you have felt in the past, you will be afraid of change if it seems to put your comfort and security—the rooms in your job—at stake. When someone comes to you with a new idea that will change your responsibility, reputation, or place in your organization, you will need special insight, confidence, and flexibility to greet the new idea warmly, rather than suspiciously. That's because, under every suspicion, lies fear. Under all fear there is a lack of confidence.

When someone wants to change your organization, *you* are at stake, not just your job or your organization. This feeling of personally being at stake applies to the chairman of the board, all the way down to the beginning manager. Contrary to the beliefs of people far down in the organization, the chairman of the board can become just as insecure as the newest employee. He just shows it differently. When the chairman becomes afraid, he uses his leverage to make sure things don't change or that they change quickly. That is why your manager, at any level, should be treated in a considerate way.

All managers are customers. They deserve to be treated as you would treat your *best* customer, no matter how good or bad your manager is. More important, *you* deserve to treat your manager as your best customer, because your approach is the key to seeing your organizational relationships become more successful than you've ever seen them before. The tremendous power of relationship becomes yours when you develop the attitude in all your dealings that *everyone you meet is your customer.* But you've got to understand what a customer really is.

Experienced sales people know that a customer isn't just someone to be sold on a preset idea of theirs, unless it is something the person really can use and benefit from. There are few farmers' daughters around any more and those who are around usually are sophisticated city people. Today's customer looks for solutions to problems, whether the customer is a woman, man, the chairman of the board, your manager, or a colleague.

When you find yourself frustrated with a problem and you finally work your way around to doing something about it—when you reach the decisive attitude—ask yourself, *Since this is my manager's problem too, how can I solve this from his perspective?* Then think of the impact on everyone else involved, and show how your solution will create a better way for everyone. If you want to change the rooms in your job, show why the change will work for everyone. Then propose a trial of thirty days or some period that allows an opportunity to try your idea without a commitment to change the organization forever. Sometimes that kind of commitment appears too unsettling to the organization.

When I started the New Perspectives program for experienced IBM employees, I announced to the marketing regions across the United States that I merely wanted to experiment with a new program and that I would run only three classes before deciding whether to continue. From the start I made it clear that the program would be voluntary. After the first class of thirteen people, little doubt remained that we had struck on something worthwhile. Three classes later, the idea had sold itself, and the program never stopped.

When you approach your manager or your peers as though they are your customers and say, "I've got something that I'm quite sure will help an older, more experienced employee stay alive and vital on the job," you've already got the attention of anyone who thinks he may have a potential problem with older employees. But you've got to close the sale.

Closing the Sale

Let's revisit an old idea for treating people as customers. It's the AIDA approach—a simple, but sound sales approach that works with anybody, managers included.

The AIDA Approach
A	Attention
I	Interest
D	Desire
A	Action

When you want to try something new or get someone else to try something new, you've got to get the attention of the person. First you've got to ask some searching questions: *What will most likely get my customer's attention?* Once you've got his or her attention, ask, *What will be of most interest? Is it organization savings, speed, or quality, or is it self-interest or some purpose the person has?* Next ask, *What would this person really* want? Remember, desire is one of the factors that changes a person's attitude around. If you don't know what the person wants and you can't figure it out, ask. Honest questions make it unnecessary to spend too much time or money on market research. Actually, questions *are* market research.

With the New Perspectives program, I just said in effect, "Here's what I'd like to do." I told them I had reserved our Sands Point facility, the most prestigious conference center in the corporation. That was the attention step. Then I said, "I guarantee you a bell-ringer program that no one will be forced to support in the future. We won't even continue it unless it turns out to be valuable." That was the interest step. Then, I asked a simple question. "Would *you* like to send someone?" That was the desire step. No mystery, no manipulation, just a question—*after* the attention and the interest steps had been taken. I offered sixteen vacancies and ended with thirteen participants. That was the action step. Later, when the program had already proven itself in the first three classes, I invited the vice-president of the division to speak.

When I spoke to the vice-president, I approached him as though he were a customer. "I've got something you ought to see," I said. After his first visit, he spoke in virtually every program I held, sometimes taking red-eye flights from the West Coast to make it to the class on time.

Attention, interest, desire, and action: This time-tested, honest, practical way works when you use it to approach anyone about anything. The trouble is, most people forget to use the approach with their own managers. Instead of treating managers as clients, employees approach them with a problem or a complaint. You can effectively deal with people above you by following this rule: *Never bring a problem to your manager without a proposal.* This works only for those who know a powerful truth: *All problems are proposals in disguise.* How do you turn a problem into a proposal? By thinking of the problem as a way to get attention, followed immediately by an intriguing idea to solve it, followed immediately by a question to determine desire, followed by a clear-cut statement of the next step you propose. But none of this should be done in a conversation alone.

Use a Visual Impact. The value of visual impact increases the likelihood of agreement, just as turbodrive increases the power of a little engine into a dynamic power generator as the car moves with accelerating speed from a red light. In an organization, for a good little idea to make a far-reaching impact, it only takes the right approach when you bring the concept to the people who have the power to decide what to do with it. Consider this for a moment:

We Retain:

    10 percent of what we read
    20 percent of what we hear
    30 percent of what we see
    50 percent of what we hear and see
    70 percent of what we say
    90 percent of what we say and do

This set of figures may vary by individual and circumstance, but they show an important principle when dealing with a good idea. *Never let a good idea down with an ineffective approach.*

Many years ago I had a manager who wanted me to present instructional material his way. I tried, but I had difficulty, and I couldn't get him to listen to me. Finally, I wrote him a letter, but instead of sending it, I brought it to him so he could read it while I stayed with him, so we could talk about it. He asked, "Why did you send me a letter when you could have just told me?"

"I *did* tell you, but my message wasn't coming through; so I thought it would help if you could see what I was saying while you hear me say it to you." All my prior discussions did not compare to this one approach. The approach paved the way for me to say, "I owe it to you to achieve the objectives of this job, and I'm committed to do that. But since I have difficulties doing the job your way, you owe it to me to let me do it a different way." Our communication was more effective from that time on, and our relationship moved from frustration to deeper awareness and to years of mutual appreciation.

Years later, along with another manager, I met with a hand-selected group of professional educators, to determine how to build a new management development program. IBM's management development had been well in place for years, including our requirement for every manager to take forty hours of management training every year. But now we faced the task of making succeeding years of training even more relevant than preceding years. It was not an easy task, and none of us knew how to do it. We had embarked on a program of skill training, rather than awareness alone, and I held the role of architect of a series of skill workshops for our managers around the world. The first meeting of our advisory board was held at a hotel in Florida, overlooking the ocean. We picked the location to signal the participants that we sought new vision and new depth of vitality in management education. We treated our board as customers.

I had gone to the best visual artist I could find and had him draw a picture of the world with a series of nine skill workshops rising out of the ocean, which would meet the needs of managers for fundamental management skills, analytical-judgmental skills, creative-innovative skills, and relationship skills. I had him draw twenty transparencies of this and other ideas that my colleagues and I felt might produce a "world-class manager." We later settled on the "excellent manager" as a more suitable title to use, and out of our effort came IBM's International Management Skill Series. But the vision caught on because we let our advisory board *see* it rather than just talking about it. We turned a problem into a proposal, and we made sure that everyone *saw* the vision while they *heard* about it—and we made sure they talked about what the vision really had to become in order to be successful.

We had no difficulty selling IBM on the idea. They were just waiting for a proposal, having already decided that management development would continue as a key to the future.

I learned, as you will, to treat everyone as my customer, including management above and people below. I learned that obtaining attention, interest, desire, and action is a good way to deal with people around you, especially when you are looking for a whole new approach that will affect the entire organization (or the entire nation, if that is your interest).

Now you need some steps for action—ways to put your new awareness to work within your organization. With the practical steps on the next pages, you'll be able to do everything we've talked about so far.

Part II

**Creating
New
Purpose
Around
You**

9

A Time for Decision

You can't pick cherries with your back to the tree.

—J. PIERPONT MORGAN

How do you move from the awareness attitude to the committed attitude with new purpose? If there truly is a new level of motivation available to you, beyond the self-interest motivation described earlier, and if this new purpose motivation is the secret to staying alive on the job throughout the rest of your career, how do you get it?

Finding New Purpose

On your road to new purpose, you'll need to take four steps. They aren't always simple to achieve, but you can easily see and understand them. You've already seen them in chapter five. Now you can begin to apply them to your search for increased vitality in your organization and your own professional life.

We might better call these four steps your four resolves:

Four Resolves to New Purpose
- To serve completely
- To believe wholeheartedly
- To recognize immediately
- To act decisively

Look below, to Illustration 11, at the seven attitudes that affect your vitality. When you reach the sixth attitude, *decisive,* exactly *what* will you do to reach the committed attitude? *How* will you reach the new purpose motivation described earlier?

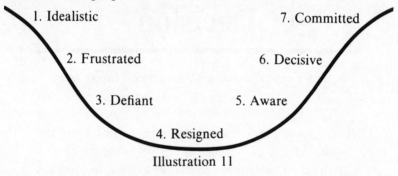

1. Idealistic   7. Committed

2. Frustrated   6. Decisive

3. Defiant   5. Aware

4. Resigned

Illustration 11

When you have reached the decisive attitude, you have reached an exhilarating crisis point. It raises your spirits because you can look forward to constructive change. In effect, you've said, "I'm going to do something about this," or "I'm going to do something about *me.*"

Earlier, when you reached the awareness attitude, you saw that you had been living in the past. That was insight. But when you reach decisiveness, you become free from the past, because of your new decision. That is resolve. But the crisis part of this happy crisis can be stated in the sobering question: To do something—what?

Take a look at the attitude curve in Illustration 12. Now you will see a sign behind the decisive attitude, much like a roadside sign that tells you to shift gears on a steep hill. This shift-gear sign must be noticed and followed, to reach the committed attitude.

How Do I Get From Decision to Commitment?

Illustration 12

The specific decisions you make along the road to commitment and new purpose are the keys to whether you get there at all. That's why the steps behind decisive are so important. Otherwise, you can slide back down the curve, jump back across the curve, or follow a number of alternatives short of reaching commitment and new purpose. These alternatives look like Illustration 13.

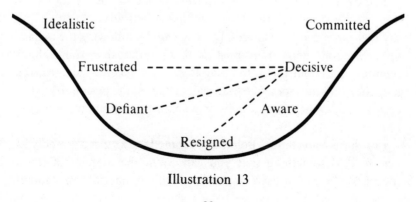

Illustration 13

Any of these alternatives can lead you into a pattern at work that looks like Illustration 14.

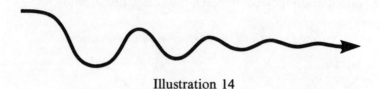

Illustration 14

Putting It Into Action

Looking again at what's behind decisiveness, you will need to work with your four steps to commitment as one decision to do all four. It won't work to take just one step or two or even three. All four go together. As you practice them in a balanced way of life at work, you will one day find yourself at the committed attitude. You may not notice when you've arrived. Someone else may see it before you do, because the committed attitude does not come from a decision or a resolve alone. It results from these, but it is different from them.

Commitment to something or to someone is the result of doing things so heartily and regularly that they become an unconscious way of life—at work or wherever you are.

Some behaviorists don't want to work with attitudes because they don't see how behavioral steps can change attitudes. Some people say you can't change attitudes, but you can, by following the behavior in the four steps. You must *do* them, rather than think about them or talk about them. In *doing* them, you become changed. It's not what goes into someone that really changes the person. It's what consistently comes from a man or woman that ultimately remakes him or her into a new person.

For those who claim, "Behavior is something you can see only in action. It is something that you can count the number of times it occurs!" listen to this: You can count the number of times someone serves in everyday work life, just as you can count the number of serves in a tennis match. You can count the number of times someone acts decisively on the job. You can count the number of times someone recognizes an act, a principle, or a person, because you can see it happen each time. You can even count the number of times an organization believes something, by the number of times it votes to take an action when it doesn't yet know how to make the action happen. In business circles that's called a strategy. A strategy board or conference does that all the time. A planning board goes a step farther and plans what ought to happen and when it ought to happen in order to make the strategy work. IBM does this every year. E. I. DuPont does this. Every enterprise that ever existed for very long has recognized the importance of moving ahead when there is no firm evidence yet that things will work out. In the same way, individuals have moments of belief when they say, "I believe I can do this," and they try. Trying is believing, and trying is observable, countable, recognizable.

Suppose for a moment that you've decided to try the four steps. You don't need to start with one prescribed step. You can start learning to recognize first, then to believe, then to serve. You can start with any one of these steps, so long as you carry on to the next until you have included all four. But one powerful principle will make the quality of your decisiveness more sure: Always determine whether you have served completely, believed wholeheartedly, recognized immediately (all three right now) before you act decisively.

It looks like this:

First these, in any order:	To serve completely
	To believe wholeheartedly
	To recognize immediately
Then this:	To act decisively

When you catch yourself about to make a decision without completing the first three steps, look back, and do those three first, and your decision will be more productive, more suitable, more creative. You will learn how to step outside your limited view of the decision and *look* at it with a new perspective.

Looking at your decisions at work with a new perspective will literally change the quality of the decision itself and in time will change you. New vitality comes from new perspective. New perspective comes from trying new things.

You need not decide now to change the rest of your entire career, unless that seems appropriate for you. Here's a short-term way to start that is workable. Consider the next thirty days as your trial month and commit yourself to practicing the four steps each day on your job. If you can apply these steps off the job, all the better, because you really can't separate vitality in one part of your life from vitality in any other part. It comes *from* you in all your walks of life.

If you count thirty days on your calendar and write your objectives, then write on tomorrow's calendar date these words, *serve completely,* then on the next day, *believe wholeheartedly,* and on the next, *recognize immediately,* and on the fourth day, *act decisively,* you will have started to be decisive. By writing these words out—in any order you choose—you will have increased the likelihood that you will do the things your own written words have said to do. It's what comes out of you, the writing of your resolve itself on thirty days of your calendar, that remarkably sets your decisiveness in gear.

Having done this, you have answered the question: "To do something—what?" Now you need to learn *how* to serve, to believe, to recognize, and to act decisively. The next four chapters will cover each of these steps by answering, "What exactly will I be doing when I follow these four steps for the next thirty days? How do I get purpose into my job and career?"

10

Serving Completely

To survive, men and business and corporations must serve.

—JOHN H. PATTERSON

A quality of selflessness brings unusual motivating power to your job, your careeer, and your life. Great leaders recognize the importance of selflessness. The public hopes for it in their elected leaders. Military and religious leaders require it. But no one really understands it until he has tried it and found the motivation it gives.

A middle-aged manager experienced it when he took two months off from work to stay at his sister's side in her final months of terminal illness. She had no family, and he felt a need to be there with her, rather than letting her lie in a nursing home, waiting to die. While he did not intend it, his credibility as a total person on the job spread quietly from his location to other locations in his national business community.

My own experience in serving came years earlier, when a young couple and their little son fled from communist Ethiopia and landed in America with no place to live and no promise of it, except for the commitment of a church in Connecticut to find a place. I came home from the office, and my wife said, "A refugee family has landed earlier than expected, and they need a place to stay for two weeks, until the right place can be found."

"All right, we'll do it," I said.

On Saturday, the uncertain father, mother, and little son stood in our kitchen with gratitude and wonder showing on their brown faces. Goitom was a good looking, young engineer. Senait was a beautiful young ray of sunshine and Biniam a dark, curly-haired, strikingly handsome little boy.

We took a walk across our little stream later that morning. When I picked up Biniam to carry him across the stream, I felt a quietly powerful message inside, saying in effect, "You are fitting into a larger purpose, and you must help." After six months of sharing our home, the little family found a place to live. Our lives had been enriched indescribably by responding to the powerful motivation to serve.

Experts in the expanding field of hospice service know that people respond to the needs of the terminally ill for personal care. Hundreds of community service organizations, such as the Lions, Rotary, Kiwanis, and others have shown that people from all walks of life have a motivation to serve others around them.

In business, some organizations, such as McDonalds, have a corporate philosophy to serve, and they are growing at an astounding rate. "We do it all for you" sells billions of hamburgers. Whether or not selfless motivation is sincere throughout an organization, service forms an essential part of our lives. IBM was built on a belief that respect for the individual, service to the customer, and excellence in everything done is an inseparable combination. General Electric's statement, "We service what we sell," creates a responsiveness in customers. An organization without a desire to serve is like a man without hands and feet, crippled in power to do what organizations must do if they wish to remain a part of our economy.

In the same way, you and I need to experience the act of serving completely. But how?

Responsiveness Versus Initiative

Before you can begin serving, you need to understand the difference between responsiveness and initiative. Both are valuable and honorable, but you need to know when to recognize and to use each. Chart 2 explains several kinds of service. Take a look at it before you go further. *Why* are positive responsiveness—carrying out the intent and precise detail of a task, when you have reason to believe it will work—and total initiative—initiating and responding to all who have a common, constructive purpose—essential as you learn to serve completely? Because you will not always know what to do in a critical or complex situation at work, and you will need to react unquestioningly and speedily at times, just as a commercial pilot must do in an instrument approach over an airport covered with heavy fog. Whether or not you act in positive responsiveness will cause the difference between success and failure, between safety and catastrophe. But you must have a confident relationship for instrument landings to work. The air traffic controller must offer total service, initiating conversation and responding to *all* the pilots intent on a common purpose of landing safely. If one pilot doesn't act with positive responsiveness, he jeopardizes all the others trying to land as well as the traffic controller, located perilously close to the landing strip.

Everyone Needs to Serve

Serving completely works well only when it works two ways, and that requires a relationship in which commitment to serve is made by management to subordinates as well as subordinates to management. It works when the team commits to help each other, rather than draw job boundaries designed to protect only one person. When you hear someone say, "That's not my job," mark it as a

Six Kinds of Service

Responsiveness			Initiative		
MALICIOUS OBEDIENCE	APATHETIC REACTION	POSITIVE RESPONSIVENESS*	SELF-SERVING	ORGANIZATIONAL	TOTAL INITIATIVE*
Doing precisely what is directed, even if you know it won't work.	Uncaring performance of the letter of the command but not considering the intent.	Carrying out the intent *and* the precise detail, *when you believe it will work.*	Initiating as well as responding, but only for your exclusive, personal gain.	Initiating and responding, but only to those in command and for mutual well-being.	Initiating and responding to all who have a common constructive purpose.

*Serving completely is practicing positive responsiveness and total initiative at the same time.

Chart 2

signal of protectionism, rather than teamwork. Uncoordinated individual protectionism in organizations doesn't work any more than it does in an instrument landing at a fogged-over airport.

When everyone in the organization commits to the idea of serving each other completely, teamwork naturally follows. But when protectionism creeps in, teamwork erodes, and total service drops off. That's when positive responsiveness erodes to apathetic reaction and finally to malicious obedience. One of the surest ways to wreck an organization or an unknowing or inexperienced manager is to *maliciously obey* by doing to the letter precisely and only what the manager says, especially when it won't work. For instance a new manager says, "Let's invite the personnel directors to our advisory board." The subordinate says, "Sure," knowing all along that the personnel directors are paid to keep the organization out of trouble, rather than find creative innovations—knowing too that certain line managers or research people would add both a strategic and creative spark. That's malicious obedience.

You might also wreck an organization by staffing it with people who would really rather move on before the needs of the organization are met. One manager remarked, "All the people here are working with their hats on!" The manager already showed the signs of frustration. Within a few months he, too, moved to the resigned attitude and left the firm.

A spirit of unwilling service spreads like the flu. Doing a job begrudgingly can never match total initiative, where people start action and respond to all the team members in a common and constructive purpose. But total initiative is a way of life that goes beyond organizational boundaries, to the edge of selflessness, and selflessness brings unusual motivating power to your life.

Put Selflessness Into Action. A young couple and their seven-year-old daughter experienced selflessness when the couple decided to bring the wife's terminally ill father home to die. Her family had been estranged from the father for many years, because of alcoholism, physical violence, and destruction; now he had no one to turn to and inadequate resources to pay for help. He had grown up in turbulence himself and had never learned how to read. The young couple had nothing to gain by taking him in, yet they had a felt need to do it.

"It was hard to do," the young mother said. "He smokes all the time, and I had to consider his effect on our daughter, but I felt we should bring him home, even though I had to resolve my old anger."

The husband said, "I felt I had received some of the good things in life at home and on the job, and I had been looking for some way to help others less fortunate in our community. It dawned on me one day that this was my way to serve. I didn't need to go somewhere else to help, when there was a need to help my own father-in-law. I found out later that the help included coming home from work and reading to my father-in-law in the evenings."

"We've been reading about Saint John," the father said one day, huddled under a shawl to keep warm. Smiling weakly, he added, "Next, we're going to read the book of Saint Joseph," not knowing there was no such book to read. In that moment, I caught a glimpse of the motivating power the young couple had felt in serving someone who had become dependent on others.

The motivating power of serving someone else completely can only be experienced and understood by trying it long enough to discover it for yourself. The desire to serve completely happens to everyone sometime in life, and you can transfer it to your job and organization life. It allows you to realize this powerful truth about staying alive *on* the job and staying vital *in* the job: *Understanding of your purpose in life* follows *your practice of serving completely.*

As you practice serving completely on the job for the next thirty days, you will find new motivation and purpose, but you will need to know the sustaining power of believing wholeheartedly. That will become more clear to you in the next chapter, because serving completely isn't enough.

11

Believing Wholeheartedly

Only so far as a man believes strongly, mightily, can he act cheerfully, or do anything that is worth the doing.

—FREDERICK W. ROBERTSON

If I say to you, "Think of the best manager you ever had and tell me what made him or her best," what will you say? Your response may vary, based on your experience over the years, but one recurring theme comes through in the variety of answers I've received.

"I could trust my manager."

"I could depend on him to tell it like it is."

"She was always honest with me."

"The best manager I had was reliable. He never let me down when I needed help."

"She was consistent. I didn't need to figure her out all the time. There was an integrity about her that made her believable."

These recurring words describe good managers: *trust, honesty, reliability, consistency.* They apply also to the things you buy and to the people you buy from. If you purchased the same brand automobile more than once, and I asked you why, what would you say? The chances are: "I trusted the company because they sold me a good car. I liked it, and I bought another."

We make strategic decisions based on our trust and belief in what has gone on before. We keep coming back to the products and people we trust. Business success is sustained not only by our products, but by customer trust in the people who produce them and will stand behind them.

You stand behind your products or services because you know that's the only way to build belief in your customers, or you do it because you believe in practicing integrity as a life-style. Either way, you know that customers return to *organizations* they believe in, even when new people run the organization. That's why organizations try to build belief into their products and into the organization itself. Sears department stores have built belief into Craftsman Tools by saying, "Anytime a Craftsman Tool breaks, bring it back, and we'll give you a new one on the spot." New York's Bloomingdales, Altman's, Macy's, and other chain stores around the nation do the same thing, as a matter of policy, because *believing in the organization ultimately sells even more products than believing in a single product itself.*

How does all this relate to *your* vitality inside your organization? If you have a commitment to do things right the first time, in addition to making things right the second time—and you hold that policy as an individual—people will believe in *you.*

If you tell me you'll make things right, I'll buy your products or service. If your organization tells me as a matter of policy that you'll *always* make things right, no matter who I deal with, I'll come to your organization first. That thought will become a habit with me, and down through the years, you will have the first chance at my business.

When you develop a reputation for performance that people can believe in, they will look your way first when the next important task comes along. But you'll need to keep up your reputation, or people will look to someone else. It can take years to build a good reputation and minutes to destroy it.

Everyone who has a good reputation also has a set of beliefs that cause the reputation. If you tell me your set of beliefs, I'll believe in you temporarily, on the condition that your performance meets the expectation you set up within me. If your performance meets that expectation again and again, you will gain my unconditional belief in you. I will believe in you wholeheartedly.

What sustains a good reputation? A set of practiced beliefs, whether they are written down and acted upon or unconsciously practiced. But you further reinforce unconscious beliefs when you write them down. For nine years I spoke at the American Management Association's premier management course in New York, San Francisco, Dallas, Chicago, Atlanta, and Toronto. In every city I asked middle-level managers to write down what they believed in when they thought of their own careers. For nine years, managers from all across the United States and Canada wrote what they believed in, because managers inherently know that behind their success lies a set of beliefs that has caused it, and they are willing to examine these beliefs as they look toward the future.

When you think of your organization or your product, what do *you* believe in? If you can't answer, you may need to find another organization or product that you can believe in.

When you think of your own strengths and aspirations, what do you believe in? If you can't think of an answer, you may need to sit down and write out the things that have made you a success as you think back over your career, because the pattern of success you have had will be the best single predictor of success for you in the future. The entire astronaut program was built on finding astronauts who believed that someone could go around the moon. They also needed astronauts who could *believe in others* on the team who would support them. Further, NASA knew when the orbit carried the astronauts around the back side of the moon, where there was no contact possible, the astronauts had to *believe in themselves* as the creators of success. If something went wrong, they had to believe they could fix it—alone. This same idea of investigating the track record of success that NASA used in selecting astronauts can work for you. Here's how. Draw a simple diagram on a sheet of paper that looks like Chart 3.

Three Major Successes

SCHOOL	CAREER	LEISURE TIME
1.		
2.		
3.		

Chart 3

Then fill in the three most significant successes you have had in each category and carry these into your future plans. This is your personal pattern of success. You can believe in it because the pattern grew out of your past and exists now.

Believing wholeheartedly is the only way to get married, the only way to form a partnership, the only way to make a career change. Half belief or three-quarter belief or temporary belief just will not do. There is only room for wholehearted, sustaining belief. Such faith motivated people to build the Erie Canal for eight long years and 250 miles across New York State, even when they ran out of money. Belief also set the path beside the Erie Canal for the New York Central railroad that opened up the Northeastern United States to the industrial development that allowed the victory of the North in the Civil War.

Sustaining belief drove the pony express and the relentless railroad gangs that followed, working their way across America from the east and west toward the golden spike, meeting in Utah. Sustained belief linked America.

Belief is not belief until it is wholehearted belief. Behind every canal, railroad, bridge, and enterprise in America there is belief. Belief isn't past tense or future tense, it is *now*. Without it, nothing gets done.

Even now as you read this, if you have faith in the sustaining power of belief, you have a spark of the same enthusiasm that created the bridges and railroads of America. Unless you have wholehearted belief in a purpose, in the possibility of *your* finding new purpose, in your own expectations for revitalization as you go, you need never start. But you *can* start, because belief is available to *you*—belief in your organization, your career, your strength, your potential. Belief is available to you within the next thirty days, but it isn't the only thing available. To serve completely and to believe wholeheartedly aren't enough. You must now learn how to recognize immediately—something the railroad organizations didn't do, and that caused their loss of vitality.

12

Recognizing Immediately

Next in importance to having good aim is to recognize when to pull the trigger.

—ELMER G. LETERMAN

For the next thirty days you can begin to experience an unusual power in your relationship at work or in any part of your life.

The secret to finding the power to recognize immediately is to learn how to make it a way of life so that you always recognize *what* is happening, *when* it happens, and *who* is making it happen. For example, you might recognize a job well done, "Fred, I saw what you did in that presentation and I liked it. The thing that worked especially well was the way you spelled out the benefits to different kinds of people in the room."

When you give that kind of *specific recognition immediately* after a presentation that Fred gives, you can guess what Fred will do next time. He will spell out the benefits to others in his very next presentation. The reason? Immediately after his success he was told what made it a success, not just, "Nice job, Fred."

Did you ever do something well but were not sure why it went so well? When someone tells you why, right away, the reason sticks with you. If too much time goes by, too many other incidents blur your ability to link up the good result with the real cause. Recognizing immediately isn't just a nice thing to do, it's the powerful thing to do. It frees a person to repeat excellence. But what about recognizing poor performance? Should you wait for a better time?

When you see a colleague has blown a presentation, the best time to recognize it, as long as you have a constructive idea, is as soon as you can get the person alone and talk about it. But you may go about it a right or a wrong way.

Here's an example: "Fred, I was watching what happened in your presentation, and I've got an idea that can help you next time. Are you interested?" If Fred isn't interested, maybe his ego has been too pounded for the moment, and you can say, "Let's have lunch tomorrow, and I'll offer you a thought that can help." Or, if Fred says, "Tell me what went wrong," you can get in a quiet corner and say, "You're so comfortable with your topic that you wanted to pack everything in the twenty minutes you had, and you blew right by your audience. They were overwhelmed. Here's how much you could have covered, and they'd have been eager for a return presentation."

Either way, immediately recognizing success *or* failure helps the other person do better. But don't do it to make *you* look good. When you recognize another's behavior, aim at helping the other person get better, not at ego boosting for either of you—but even that good purpose can be taken too far.

Did you every run across someone who always wanted to tell you what *you* did wrong, but never wanted to know from you how he or she did? Recognition is a two-way street. It works better when you both agree to give honest feedback immediately, but with respect for the feelings of each other. This honest reflection becomes a helpful mirror for each, so that *both* of you will learn how to get better. You need to use it to get at the cause of strength and the cause of weakness—not just try to make someone feel good. Often those who do it try to use it as a tactic to make people like them, even though that's hard to admit and such a person usually doesn't even recognize that motivation. Deep down, everyone can appreciate real honesty, if it's offered out of caring for their good.

Years ago, a secretary who worked for me didn't realize that she was judgmental of others in the department. Although she was attractive, bright, articulate, and competent, her attitude turned people off. When we talked about it, I asked, "Have you noticed some people aren't responding to your suggestions?"

"Yes," she said, "and I don't understand it."

"What you are telling them is correct. But it's the *way* you tell them that isn't working."

"What am I doing?" she asked, looking at me intently. She had moved from attention to interest. The next step was to find her desire to learn how to fix it—the next step in the AIDA approach.

"I think you are standing on a pedestal, figuratively, and you are speaking down to your colleagues. Sometimes that means you show a touch of judgment in your manner or in the spirit of your advice. Often people can't even detect a judgmental manner in words alone, nor can a person who gives the advice, but it happens anyway. For instance, it could be happening to me right now."

I looked at her carefully, reminding myself that I wanted to help her, not set her straight, and I wanted to remove any distance I might have caused. "Am I being helpful to you right now?"

"Yes," she said.

"For the next thirty days, would you like to have a little pact between us that may help?"

"Yes, I think so."

"All right, when I notice in a meeting or conversation that you are having with someone that they are getting turned off, I'll pull on my ear, like this. That will signal you that something just happened. I may not even know what happened, but at least we'll both know *something* happened. If you'll take note of what you've just said and your own motivation for saying it, at that moment, we'll talk later, as soon as we can do that privately."

"Will you do that for me?" she asked, showing in her face that she appreciated the idea of our pact.

"I will, if you'll do the same for me."

"It's a deal," she said, with a big smile. Years later, she came to me when she was a second-level manager and invited me to talk to her group about handling stressful relationships. Her way of speaking to others had been the single most limiting thing in her personal and career growth, and our agreement together to recognize something immediately turned out well.

To recognize immediately, caringly—for the benefit of the other person and not yourself—frees up people to look at the cause of success or failure. By entering into a two-way agreement where each willingly helps the other with honest feedback, both are helped to new power. Your skills get better, and so does your relationship. But your words must be honest, and your manner must be caring. And it helps powerfully when you both focus on the cause or on why you're doing something. That's real recognition. Aim not just at saying something nice—that can become sickeningly sweet at best and manipulative at worst—but aim at helpfulness.

The freeing power of recognizing immediately becomes yours when you simply find a receptive colleague and say, "I've got something to improve that I'd like to work on, and I wonder if you will let me know when I'm missing the boat. If you'll do that for me for the next thirty days, I'll do the same for you."

Try it for a month. It works—just as serving completely works and believing wholeheartedly works. But these three purposes work better when you practice them together. That way one purpose doesn't get overused and out of hand. But you also need to learn to act decisively and creatively.

13

Acting Decisively

The great use of life is to spend it for something that outlasts it.

—WILLIAM JAMES

What does it take to make creative decisions quickly and accurately? Have you made them well in the past? If not, perhaps it comes from the fact that most of your life you've been trained, prodded, or cultured to make a decision without the creative power of the first three steps we've already studied. Creative decisions result from something far more than your ability to add a series of figures or mentally calculate the impact of several choices. Let's see how to serve, believe, recognize, and act decisively for a more vital career!

Achieving Personal Vitality

In speaking on career planning across the United States and in foreign countries, I have found, much to my surprise, that most adults have left many of their career decisions to their companies or to someone else. Somehow they feel they get paid to make decisions for the company, but not to make them for their future career vitality. As a result, they lose their energy, and their organizations lose a powerful resource.

When I consulted for Kenneth J. Burk, senior vice-president of a major insurance corporation, I submitted a plan to help people in his company make personal career-vitality decisions. We published a self-decision manual that was used successfully by both managers and nonmanagers. We began it with a provocative statement adapted from an advertisement by a New York advertising firm:

How to Retire at Thirty-five

It's easy. Thousands of people do it every year. In all walks of life.

And it sets our economy, our country, and the world back thousands of years in terms of wasted human resources. But worst of all is the personal tragedy that almost always results from "early retirement."

It usually begins with a tinge of boredom. Gradually a person's work begins to seem endlessly repetitious. The rat race hardly seems worth it anymore. It's at this point that many a 35-year-old boy wonder or girl wonder retires. There are no testimonial dinners or gold watches.

He or she stills goes to work every day, puts in forty hours, and even draws a paycheck. He or she has retired, but nobody knows it. Not at first, anyhow.

The lucky ones get fired in time to make a fresh start. Those less fortunate hang on for a while—even decades—waiting and wondering. Waiting for a raise or promotion that never comes, and wondering why.

There are always ways to fight back, though, and most people do. They counteract the urge to coast by running as they've never run before. They run until they get the second wind that is known as "self-renewal."

Self-renewal is nothing more or less than doing for yourself what your parents, teachers, coaches, and bosses did for you when you seemed young enough to need it. It's the highest form of self-discipline. And it can be one of the most satisfying experiences a person can enjoy.

Self-renewal is the adult's ability to motivate himself, to reawaken self-pride in the face of spiritual fatigue. Self-renewal is the device by which the boy wonders become men and girl wonders become women. They become leaders. Creators. Thinkers. Self-renewal is probably the greatest test a business person must face.

It's worth the effort, though. With life expectancy approaching the century mark, sixty-five years is a long time to spend in a rocking chair.

This clearly made the point that, to experience a new depth of vitality, you will need to look at your career and your life in depth.

Getting Control

On the surface, your career appears as a series of jobs, stretching over a lifetime. But they can seem disconnected and lack a bridge from one to the next that makes real impact. How can you take a clear look at your career vitality?

Beneath your past and future lies a driving force that makes a series of jobs into a career. This force is made of four inseparable but very individual forces we have been considering: your willingness to serve, your capacity to believe, your ability to recognize immediately, and your readiness to act decisively and creatively. You can put these driving forces to work for you by establishing a few key objectives for obtaining added skills.

You have brought some interests and skills into each job you have held and taken them from each job into the next. But if you haven't explored your individual purpose and refined your skills to carry it out, or if you haven't even focused on them, you have already accepted someone else's decisions on what your career and life ought to be. Your purpose and your skills together should be the basis for your decisions. Sometime in your life it becomes clear that unless you invest *yourself*—really put all your total purpose consciously into the decisions of your life—someone else will make your career and life decisions for you, based on their needs alone.

The way to a more successful career and life is to focus on your purpose and skills, both past and present, and project them into your future. In that way future jobs or expansion of your present job will come from your state of readiness. In this way your own purpose, which you clarified in your first three steps, will become a powerful motivating force, pulling you into your future.

You can play a bigger role in your own future vitality. By developing what you *should* be doing with your career and life, now—no matter how long you've been working or how successful you are at the moment.

Personal Vitality Questions

As you have seen throughout this book, *you* are the key to more productive career vitality discussions in the future. But how do you get started?

Throughout this book you have read about the power of questions to help you discover new vitality. Now you can practice this "question power" on your own career decisions by using the following vitality inventory in a discussion with a person you select, sometime within the next thirty days. This is designed to help you push out the walls of your life and to help you act more decisively and creatively.

1. What purpose are you committed to as a person?
2. What is one thing you stand for and believe in as a person?
3. What is your real strength at this point in your life?
4. Do you have a personal goal to achieve or service that you want

to perform in life—something that needs to be done or changed or eliminated? If you do, what is it?

5. Are you interested in a specific job, either in or out of your organization, that requires skills you do not possess? If you do, what is it? What specific skills does the job require, as you now view it?

6. Do you have one or more additional skills in mind that you want to develop? If so, what are they?

7. How do you utilize the three steps—to serve completely, to believe wholeheartedly, to recognize immediately—to increase the power of your fourth step: drawing on the decisive power of purpose within you?

The Next Step Is Yours

Whether or not you intended it, you now have a better feeling for vitality—what it is, how to get it, how to keep it. Vitality on the job is inseparable from vitality off the job. And the chances are you've got it in a fuller measure than you did when you started this book. That is, if you really are doing something different.

What you've been doing here is not just thinking about vitality or talking about a career. As said in the beginning of this chapter, "With the life expectancy approaching the century mark, sixty-five years is a long time to spend in a rocking chair." Who really wants to retire, anyway, when there's so much to do, so much to learn, so much to be?

The key is to do something different. Not necessarily in a different place or in a different job, though that's often a good idea. The key is to do something different right where you are—something creative, something helpful.

One way to be sure you are enjoying your life and your career is to get into the present with both feet. Get out of yesterday and tomorrow. Don't become obsessed with either one. Today is. And today is the day to start doing something different. Standing beside Thomas Watson, Jr., one day at IBM's corporate management development center, I listened as he gave me some advice. I had watched his career since 1956, through his years as IBM chairman of the board and as ambassador to Russia. Now in retirement, he was speaking to me—and to you. "I don't like to think of anyone looking back in life," he said. "It's such a waste."

Are you still sitting down? This is your opportunity to commit yourself to someone else. In the next thirty days you can write out some answers to the questions in this chapter, then meet with a friend for advice. You can say to someone what you would like to do, then commit yourself to that person that you are going to take the first step. That's practicing decisiveness.

When you become decisive—and not until you do—you will make an impact on your organization.

Part III

Learning From Others Who Have Used the Keys to Professional Vitality

Part III

14

The
Power
of
Decisiveness

Knowing is not enough; we must apply. Willing is not enough; we must do.

—GOETHE

We met in Frank Pace's sprawling office in midtown Manhattan. A picture window took up the entire wall and displayed a sweeping view from the Empire State Building down to the World Trade Center Towers and the lower New York Bay. This panorama of buildings seems a suitable background for the mission of a man with a driving purpose and an infectious smile that makes you feel comfortable in an instant as he walks around his office telling you stories about the presidents of the United States he has served. Frank Pace was secretary of the army during World War II.

"Of the six presidents, Nixon, Ford, Johnson, Kennedy, Eisenhower, and Truman, one stands out above all the rest for his sense of leadership."

"Which one is that?" I asked, trying to guess quietly. *Was it Eisenhower? Kennedy?* I wondered.

"Harry Truman stands above all the rest," Frank Pace said. "He, more than any others, *understood* the presidency. He used to say, 'There are many others more capable than I. But there is only one president. And the office itself commands that attention and responsiveness needed to lead the United States!' President Truman respected the presidency and required everyone to do the same. His decisiveness came from his unique understanding of what his job really was and how to use the job to get things done."

Sitting in Frank Pace's office, on his spacious couch, with his memories of public life surrounding us, I saw how important it is for a president to push out the walls of his position, and I sensed the spontaneous enthusiasm of Frank Pace as he talked about the great military leaders he worked with: Marshall, Eisenhower, MacArthur, Bradley. Grinning, he told me, "Patton used to say, 'I'd rather face an entire Nazi panzer division than have an interview with George Catlett Marshall.' " Now, leaning toward me from his wingback chair, Frank Pace warmed to his favorite topic. "The secret is individual leadership," he said. "What this country desperately needs is to understand what leadership really is. More than that, we need to learn how to teach it, in our high schools, colleges, and business organizations. We know a good deal about management, but we don't know enough about leadership."

While Frank Pace spoke, I could feel the vitality of a man twenty years older than me, who clearly was a leader, as he urged me to push out the walls of understanding so that Americans could recapture the enthusiasm for leadership we once had. I couldn't yet define why I liked Frank Pace, I just knew that I did, instantly, and that my appreciation for the man deepened as we went on.

"Theodore Roosevelt was a remarkable leader," Frank continued. "He knew long ago that we had foisted upon ourselves an unrealistic wage scale that ultimately would choke our ability to compete abroad." Again Frank leaned forward. "We must be individuals in our work. And we must make middle management and blue-collar work more attractive, rather than rely on monetary policies to keep us strong. One of the places to start is with our white-collar middle managers, because they have become the real blue-collar workers of today. In the competitive process of United States business, our strength lies in finding a simple but workable answer to individual leadership in our lives, as workers, managers, and parents." Frank Pace's commitment never flagged as he spoke of a subject that he obviously believed in deeply.

"Can American workers establish enough internal purpose to regain our historic ability to compete?" Frank looked at me squarely now, enlisting my intellectual support for reestablishing a missing requirement of our society.

"I've had a long and rewarding career," he said, "and it's not over. I've been dealt a handful of aces, and every time I discard one, someone hands me another. Now I'm interested in helping my country. It's been good to me, and it needs help. If America is to remain competitive over the years, without protectionism, we must work from the inside out.

"The key to our national future is to find organizations that will make the effort to gradually change their internal culture to permit controlled leadership *at every level.*"

We talked at length then of new vitality inside people and organizations, and our conversation continued in other meetings in Frank Pace's Greenwich, Connecticut, home, where I saw him as a devoted family man with his wife, Peg, sharing a vitality in life, undergirded by a strong sense of purpose in their lives, and balanced by a strong devotion to each other. We talked of the two questions from the New Perspectives program: "What is important?" and, "Who is important?"

"For me, the questions are, 'What is essential?' and 'Who is essential?' Don," Frank said in his living room one Saturday morning. "In America today we have a responsibility to those we lead, and we have the responsibility to maintain sound values. Voltaire said it well: 'Freedom is only the opportunity for self-discipline.' When you follow that thought and let it become part of you, then you begin to experience the glories of leadership, where one of the essentials is self-discipline."

As I came to know and appreciate Frank Pace over the months of sharing our mutual interests, I began to see that his vitality comes from a committed attitude and unquenchable sense of purpose.

"I'm afraid I'm a confirmed workaholic," he said one Saturday, sitting with another set of historic memoirs surrounding him. "I like work," he said. "I seldom take a vacation—I suppose because I have a vision of what we can still do for America. My organization is dedicated to helping executives find ways to lead American business back into leadership again. It may take a long time, but I'm willing to give as much time as I have."

Frank Pace has an organizational vision for America in his current job as chairman of the National Executive Service Corps where he serves at no salary and donates the rental costs. "Unless we as companies see our new leadership role, we will never achieve our national purpose. We must find it in our business environment. We must take risks and innovate at a corporate level, or we will slowly lose our economic vitality as a nation. We have become a special-interest society, and we can't afford to be. We need people who can lead us out of special interests into common interests, and we've got to do that by appealing to the minds *and* hearts of people, not just to their minds.

"Another field that requires our national focus is education. In our state universities, ninety-five percent of the curriculum is oriented to the mind, and only five percent to the heart.

"In our larger private colleges, eighty-five percent of the curriculum is oriented to the mind and fifteen percent to the heart. Our community colleges are oriented seventy percent to the mind and thirty percent to the heart. In our smaller, private colleges, the orientation is sixty percent to the mind and forty percent to the heart. And in them we are on the right track, because leadership—believe it—is eighty percent *heart* and twenty percent *mind.*

"When you look at what chief executive officers say is the distinguishing characteristic of a CEO, they ask, 'Can he be a leader?' When you think of that and the fact that attitude and productivity are more related than any other combination, you are drawn toward two additional questions: 'What is the corporation's responsibility for attitude? What is the cost of *not* creating an attitude of leadership, at all levels?' "

I was clearly caught up with the searching questions Frank Pace had asked and by the flow of ideas whenever we met, because this man practices leadership instinctively, while he talks about it. He has lived it in public life for the major part of his career. His experience with leadership in the key army role he played during history's biggest war reveals powerful insights in the success of military organizations and the part that leadership plays.

"We have a principle in the army, that the soldier should eat first. That is backed up by an abiding belief that the army is run by the noncommissioned officers, not by the generals. In view of that, I believe it is unwise of us to believe that we cannot improve leadership at all levels in American business. Further, we need leaders in every walk of life: the family, community, state, and nation. Great leaders must be prepared to face their particular futures, but they must be ethical, honest, caring people, and they must be agents of considered change."

As I listened to Frank Pace, I felt that he spoke with conviction because he has a commitment to a future purpose. All his motivation seems based upon this purpose. His views come close to John Gardner's comments, published in *Harper's Magazine* in October, 1965: "Most organizations have a structure that was designed to solve problems that no longer exist," and, "An organization runs on motivations, on conviction, on morale." Frank Pace's vitality comes from purpose motivation, rather than self-interest motivation. His committed attitude shows in everything he says, yet his warmth is real in every conversation.

His special insight on presidential success can help you, whatever your level, as he describes the importance of decisiveness. Here is Frank Pace's perspective on the nine most important decisions of Harry Truman, a common man who became one of America's most respected and decisive presidents:

No one has ever fully exposed the remarkable qualities of President Truman as a leader. When you consider the limited quality of background experience he brought to the presidency, his performance appears quite exceptional. Suddenly thrust into the position, with little warning and no preparation, Truman yet made these important decisions that influenced the course of history.

1. He decided how to terminate the war in Japan. In guiding him on this first and one of the most substantial challenges of his career, his joint chiefs of staff recommended invasion. "How many American lives would it cost?" asked Mr. Truman. The answer: "300,000 to 400,000." "How many Japanese lives?" The answer came back: "Over a million." "That," said Mr. Truman, "is not acceptable." He based the decision to use the atom bomb on its minimal impact on life and property.

2. He chose to give the defeated enemy considerate treatment after World War II. (This action ran so contrary to Joseph Stalin's nature that some effective persuasion had to come into play. Knowing Stalin's dislike for Winston Churchill, Frank Pace asserts that President Truman played the effective middleman and achieved the desired results.)

3. Truman decided to preserve Berlin by airlift, rather than by attacking along the corridor. Frank Pace states that the wisdom of this has never been challenged.

4. The president decided to establish a boundary of United States

support for Greece and Turkey against Russian incursion, preserving the existence of those two nations.

5. Truman supported the creation of NATO, with all its implications for preserving peace in Europe over forty years and for making Europe a major link in free-world defense.

6. President Truman signed the legislation that put the Marshall Plan into effect, insuring the economic solvency of Europe after World War II.

7. Truman supported the controversial creation of the State of Israel, when it became apparent that a home for the Jewish people had to be established.

8. He decided to bring the United States into the Korean War. One week later the United Nations voted to send its forces into the conflict.

9. Truman chose not to use the atom bomb when our soldiers were being threatened by overwhelming Chinese forces during the Korean War.

These nine important decisions of Harry Truman point up the value of acting decisively, the fourth step to commitment. To act decisively and creatively is a key to personal and organizational commitment, and this forms a significant part of Frank Pace's secret for staying vital. He learned how to serve six presidents—and America—completely. He believes wholeheartedly in the need for leadership. He has acquired the ability to immediately recognize the skills of people around him and to encourage them to achieve to the limit of their current ability and sometimes beyond it. But most important, he has learned to act decisively when he sees a new idea.

You can incorporate these same skills in your organization as you reflect on the decisiveness of Frank Pace and the beliefs that have made him a successful leader.

15

The Power of Recognizing Your Opportunities

Opportunity is ever worth expecting; let your hook be ever hanging ready, the fish will be in the pool where you least imagine it to be.

—ANONYMOUS

We were high above New York's prestigious Park Avenue, as it stretched into uptown Manhattan, into the gathering dusk of the city's twilight haze. As millions of Manhattan lights gradually switched on in the growing darkness below, Bill Kanaga and I talked about personal motivation, organization vitality, and the future.

Bill Kanaga looked forward to retirement from his position as chairman of Arthur Young, one of the big eight international accounting, tax, and consulting organizations in the United States. Arthur Young's array of services provide sound financial, accounting, and tax consultation on one side and expert advice in many areas of management, including innovation, on the other. Together, these balanced offerings provide an opportunity for a company and an individual to be aware of the opportunities of the future.

Bill and I sat in his executive conference room at the close of his last day as chairman of the Arthur Young organization. The staff had gone home. The corridors were dimmed for the evening, and the air conditioning had been turned off. At this special moment, the rush of years of work seemed suspended, waiting for the wisdom gleaned from the past to recognize the opportunities of the future. How do you maintain vitality when one career is over and a new life is just now ready to begin? What new opportunities can you make out of a pinnacle of past success?

We talked first about the unusual nature of large accounting organizations, specifically of the Arthur Young organization, really a large partnership with 750 partners among a work force of 8,500 people across the United States and a worldwide organization of 25,000 people in seventy countries. One of every eleven people in the United States organization is a partner, working in one of eighty offices, focused on the financial centers of New York, Chicago, Los Angeles, and Dallas, and in all major regional and local centers of the country.

"Why a partnership organization?" I asked, wondering about the concept of purpose motivation.

"A fundamental advantage of a partnership is that it changes the standard pyramid structure of the corporate organization. It becomes something that looks more like a double funnel with the narrow ends meeting and the open ends providing a widening flow of opportunity at the bottom and innovation at the very top." Bill spoke enthusiastically about a major problem facing industry and about a potential breakthrough in organizational vitality. The difference looks something like Illustration 15:

The Standard Organizational Pyramid

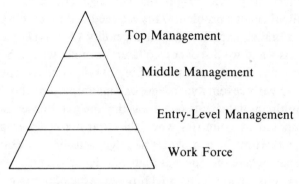

The Partnership Funnel

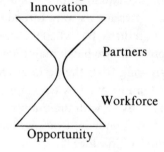

Illustration 15

"With 750 partners in our organization, we find that each person actually constructs the job he or she lives in in an entrepreneurial way by changing the broad framework of the job. We want each partner to live and breathe in a fresh way. We think this creates a positive turbulence in the firm that generates new ways to improve upon our services to our markets.

"We limit the tenure of a partner in a given spot by changing the job opportunities periodically. No one should feel he has his job locked in. The flexibility of changing our partners' roles every five years or so helps them to be revitalized and helps us to be more innovative as an organization. We have established coordinating roles where one partner brings together several others to work on an individual client's problem. This is a seed bed that allows us to tap into the brains, experience, and ingenuity of our people to find solutions—and we discover a collateral benefit, where they are not proprietary, that the solutions apply to other clients around the world.

"Nearly seventy years ago, one major personnel problem that our multinational clients faced was the unequal burden of income taxes imposed by countries when they transferred international assignments. How the companies handled transfers, for example, between Japan, where the rate was high, and Hong Kong, where the rate was low, was a major personnel problem. One of our partners saw working in this area of 'tax equalization' as a major opportunity. Many of our young tax professionals were turned off to the idea of working on personal tax returns; but when we worked out a motivational solution to that problem, we had a major new and successful service product, really growing from the germ in one partner's mind."

"Bill," I said, "I'm intrigued by the counterbalancing of financial accounting and tax advice with the innovation consulting that your organization does. Did your innovation management services grow out of the tax-equalization idea?"

"Not really. One of our partners, Cesar Pereira, became interested in innovation itself as a fine opportunity for us. He brought in Austin Pryor, who had extensive background and experience in corporate venturing and innovation; and he persuaded Bill Foster, president of the Institute for Innovation and a leader in the new field of innovation consulting, to become associated with us. From the combined ideas of these people we're offering an emerging area of service that combines our financial experience with innovation management consulting. Cesar Pereira became the chairman of our Innovative Management group because he wasn't afraid of fostering a new idea. It's this kind of responsible risk taking that we encourage internally that helps us expand the ways we help our clients. With the tax equalization idea, some people said, 'This is too small a market area.' But those who believed in it pressed on and showed that a major market existed."

"What we like to see is people who say, 'See this,' to others around them. That's our way of building teamwork here. We like people to bounce their ideas off others. We give extra points to partners who check out their ideas before passing them on to a client. We try to encourage our partners to recognize opportunities but to recognize the realities at the same time. We encourage people not to be loners, not only in current client problem solving but also where new business ventures are involved. If people are not consumed by worry over who gets the credit, there is no limit to what an organization such as ours can achieve.

"But what makes partnership really work, Bill?" I asked, thinking of purpose motivation.

"Enthusiasm makes it work," Bill responded. "Give people what they like to do and enough room to do it in and the sky is the limit. Obviously, management has to manage, to measure these against the resources we have available."

"What has kept you enthusiastic in your career, Bill, now that you've reached your last day?"

"For me, it's changing responsibilities and opportunities. With the chairmanship of Arthur Young now behind me, I'll be able to do more on the boards I am serving. Each new board and new activity calls on new skill areas. I'll work on the board of the United States Chamber of Commerce and on the centennial celebration of the United States accounting profession, among others. I'll probably do different things, but in the same way I have been doing them. I've found over the years that you've got to get out of your chair and understand what your real job is. You've got to walk the territory, even if that means riding the delivery truck of your client. When you get out where the service is being performed, you gain an understanding and become enthusiastic."

"But how does that work for people throughout the organization?" I asked.

"That's exactly where I learned it—as a young manager. We have to encourage managers to foster the growth of subordinates, so they will be pushed and have the same skill when they become managers."

"How did that work for you, Bill?"

"A partner I worked for always kept me feeling like my head was just barely above the water. I was always stretched to the limit. That's a need of the organization—to keep people stretched. They love that. We can't allow complacency, or all of us will drown.

"I've looked at the seven attitudes you talk about, Don. They can be managed by an 'up or out' policy. You get to be a partner, or you move on to another organization. Historically in Arthur Young we'd like all our career people to become partners or principals in highly specialized areas. Then we can move them from responsibility to responsibility to keep them vital."

"What are the early warning signs that people are losing their vitality?" I asked.

"When there are no vital relationships with clients. Sometimes this appears when there are problems in collecting fees, but the real problem has begun earlier, when there is a lack of attention to service. We foster autonomy in order to serve the client completely, but we also assess the overall vitality of an office along the way, because that's a mirror of the vitality of the partners in it."

"What are the keys to success in vitality, Bill?"

"Maximum service in the minimum response time."

"But how do you balance this with family life?"

"Frankly, I've found when your family life is out of balance, the flywheel isn't working. One of the keys to long-term success is to recognize out-of-balance situations. That's a key to maintaining long-term performance. You've got to balance your family and your organization. In any firm, the executives must understand that balance is important for the long run."

"But people at work don't often see this family balance encouraged, Bill."

"That's why I'm convinced that executives should be real in the speeches they make, and those speeches have to reflect reality of behavior. We should be real people both at work and at home. And we should talk about the need for balance. In my life, I saw that my world was a little like a doughnut. At one point I was made aware that there was a hole in my life that God has filled for me."

"Bill, what are the most critical problems facing business in America today?"

"One of them deals with the same thing we've been talking about. In American business life one of our weakest points is recognizing the importance of family life. In business, we haven't done well in communicating the value of the same integrity that works in our families. Dealing with others as we would like to be dealt with is a key.

"Another critical problem is the fact that sometimes communities don't recognize that business wants *long-term* results. Where business thinks in the short-term only, it is in trouble. Business must become a leader in raising the general level of morality in American life."

We had been talking about recognizing your opportunities in career life and organizational life. On this last day of the month and last day of Bill's job as chairman, following a career based upon the special strength of the accounting profession, of recognizing opportunities and potential problems before it's too late, I searched for more insight on purpose motivation.

"What is your purpose, Bill, now that you've reached a special place in your life?"

"I'm going to take on some new responsibilities right here," he said. "I'll be chairman of an advisory board we are establishing, but beyond that, I know I don't want to be a spectator in life. If I think I can make a difference, then I want to be a part of the purpose and the organization that wants to make a difference."

"And *your* purpose?"

"To use my God-given talents to make our world a better place. I ask God for wisdom and help, and He has supported and strengthened me."

These are words of motivation, responsibility, and innovation for Bill Kanaga, at the top. Now I was interested in the organization below Bill Kanaga, beyond Arthur Young's experience in financial, accounting, tax and management consulting, at the service of innovation consulting. Cesar Pereira's innovation experts, Austin Pryor and Bill Foster, had become one of the innovative teams Bill Kanaga and Cesar Pereira sought. During dinner I asked them about innovation.

Bill Foster, spoke first. "You've got to look at your attitude toward failure. To be innovative, you can't be frightened of failure. Every three hundred hitter in baseball is really a practitioner of prudent failure." Bill went on to say that every leading batter does what every true leader does. Leaders and batters *always* take risks.

"There are three levels of people in organizational life," Bill went on. "There are corporate sky divers, corporate custodians, and corporate followers." Bill Foster's comment fit in with my own belief that we make sky divers into custodians when we require perfection of the sky divers. But striving for controlled perfection in everything ultimately causes mediocrity in the organization, because most of the effort gets bureaucratically focused on the means, not the end. People become very good at what they do, but they may never do what is important.

Bill Foster continued. "Some companies are like that, too. They never look for the long pass. These are often the failure companies. The success companies go around the walls of resistance. They step back and look at themselves—at who they are and what they are doing. Then they look for a way around the wall—or a pass over it.

"There are five primary ways that a company manages itself: through plans, structure, culture, policies and programs, and through practice. We have learned these ways primarily from the manufacturing heritage of business. But now, with our service-dominated economy, we need to move from a *manufacturing*—"make with hands"—to a *mentafacturing*—"make with mind"—mentality.

While most companies are being driven into the future by looking in a rearview mirror—the old manufacturing view of how to manage—we're advocating using the concept of mentafacturing to drive us into the future by looking out the *front* window. One way you do that is by giving employees more opportunities not only to think innovatively, but to do something about their thoughts.

I thought of the New Perspectives Program during our conversation and we discussed this. The idea of encouraging professional leaders at all levels seemed to fit in with Bill Foster's comments. Bill went on to talk about attitudes.

"General Montgomery used to say it was the attitude of his troops that made a key difference. I agree, and I add a question about the organization's attitude, too. Does the *organization* want to be a leader? There is a definite 'attitude wave' about innovation coming. We've seen it in our joint study conducted by Arthur Young, the Institute for Innovation, and the Foresight Group. We asked 400 United States companies what is necessary to encourage innovation, and the message is clear."

"Improve the management environment by top-management innovation and leadership—visually and financially—with continuity and commitment." I thought of Bill Kanaga's comments and the Arthur Young climate of innovation. They seemed to fit.

"The Golden Rule works at the company level, too," Bill Foster continued. "You've got to service the needs of all your clients or customers. And on an individual level it's becoming clear that successful people, over time, are service oriented."

"But what about failure of the top management? What causes that?" I asked. Bill had three phrases I have highlighted here:

- Complacency
- Fear of failure
- Arrogance

"Fear is a mental disease," Bill said.
That rang a bell with me. "But what about faith?" I asked.

"Where does that fit in? In my view, fear is the opposite of faith."

"Spiritual concepts like faith are coming back," Bill said. "Culture has always been important. We've just begun to recognize it again.

"In Portugal's prime, their ship captains were willing to sail off the edge of the world, in a day when the maps showed dragons at the end of the known seas. What we're doing now is learning how to go further than our traditional thoughts and our fears will let us. Our research shows that 70% of the innovation barriers are barriers of the mind. Look at Portugal today. As a nation of former explorers, now they seemed entrapped, resigned to their fate. What Portugal primarily needs to regain their explorer mentality is to change their attitude.

"Plato had a good comment when he said, 'What you honor, you cultivate.' Take a look at our Jewish contribution to the list of Nobel prize winners. Eighty percent are Jewish. What would happen over time if these people were to change the things they honor?

"Now let's look at our business future in America. The real growth in recent years has been in the mid-sized companies, not in the biggest companies. What we continually need to look for are *breakthroughs in business.* We need people and organizations who haven't recognized that it can't be done."

Bill went on. "Real leaders aren't afraid to be slightly crazy. In fact, the most important quality of a real leader is that he or she isn't afraid to stand alone. Real leaders have vision, faith, and willingness to strike out."

I thought of the Jewish heritage again as Bill Foster spoke. Moses and Joshua could teach us lessons in leadership today—how to set goals and stick with them, regardless of popular sentiment.

"All *major* innovations appear dumb in the beginning," Bill was saying. "Now we are willing to pay for overnight delivery, Xerography, and Zap Mail. But before they became regular services, how many people would have invested heavily in these as a real business opportunity?"

"What are the characteristics of good management in your own lives?" I asked Bill Foster and Austin Pryor. The answer both agreed upon was basic, yet powerful, to me:

- Extraordinary respect for the individual
- Openness to unusual and creative thinking of strong mavericks
- A climate where you can talk about what you tried and failed to achieve

"What about the *worst* managerial characteristics?" I asked.

"Rule by fear or humiliation and a short-term perspective," Austin Pryor responded.

"What would you say to your son or daughter who wants to do well in the career world?" This time the advice was less familiar but equally sound:

- Throw away your preconceived notions of how things ought to be done. Get a clear vision of what you want to be
- Be willing to do something very different
- Be realistic about your strengths and weaknesses and never stop trying to grow

As we drew to a close, a further word of advice seemed consistent with all that had been said by Bill Kanaga at the top and by Bill Foster and Austin Pryor in the innovation group. "Don't look for magic Band-Aid answers," they said. "Most answers are fundamental. People say 'That's obvious,' then they don't act on the obvious." But when they do they find, as the Arthur Young Institute for Innovation Management Group has, that hiding inside every company is *enormous* innovative and entrepreneurial potential. Our task is to recognize, then unleash, the power that exists within. But recognizing alone isn't enough. We need implementation. We need to learn more about what it means to serve completely. For that we will look at another leader.

16

The Power
of
Serving
Completely

If there be any truer measure of a man than by what he does, it must be what he gives.

—ROBERT SOUTH

Sitting in the Showboat Restaurant, in Greenwich, Connecticut, with President Kennedy's yacht, *The Honey Fitz,* tied up at the dock just outside, I renewed an acquaintance with Gene Cooper, whom I had met years earlier in Denver. We had met just once, but our friendship had grown by telephone since our meeting, and I had come to realize that Gene Cooper, at seventy-eight, had learned a secret for staying vital. Somewhere in Gene's life, he developed a purpose that shows in his dealings with strangers and old friends alike. With three

137

degrees, in chemistry, engineering, and law, with experience as the owner of his own successful firm and as a private pilot of his own plane, I felt Gene Cooper had not only learned some powerful lessons about revitalizing himself but he could help others, too.

Years before, when I landed in Denver, Gene met me at Stapleton International Airport, and we drove north toward Cheyenne. Along the way, we spotted a car pulling off to the side, smoke pouring out from the rear-wheel well. We pulled over and tried to help by getting buckets of water from a stream, but within minutes the car broke out in flames and was consumed before the family could retrieve any of their belongings. The young couple and their three shoeless children stood by the highway in the summer sun, looking at their car and all their possessions, burned beyond use. We returned momentarily to our car, and Gene said, "I've got a hundred-dollar bill that I keep for emergencies. I'm going to loan it to them and see if there is a place for them to stay while I get you to Cheyenne." Gene Cooper arranged all that in minutes, and I became more intrigued by this person who had volunteered to drive me to Cheyenne and had helped a stranded family along the way.

Now, sitting in the restaurant, I probed Gene's secret of vitality.

"I sold my firm years ago, when my wife became an invalid. She needed constant care, and I decided that she needed me more than I needed my company. I've been caring for her since."

Knowing Gene has been a recovered alcoholic for forty-five years, I asked him how he had accomplished his "celebration of sobriety," as he called it.

"Maybe I'm stubborn," he said. "Or maybe it's been the things I learned through Alcoholics Anonymous." I probed further for secrets in this part of his life.

"I am one of the original 300 members of Alcoholics Anonymous," he told me. "I was one of the committee members who returned a quarter-million-dollar donation from Anheuser-Busch."

Surprised, I asked, "Wasn't that hard to do?"

"No, it wasn't. Years ago, our organization developed a strong belief that we must survive without outside help. Now, that belief is in our bloodstream as an organization. We saw the need for this kind of organizational resolve almost from the beginning. It's born of the same resolve our individuals must have."

"How did Alcoholics Anonymous come about?" I asked. I was intrigued with the explosive growth and obvious vitality of that group across the United States. It seemed to me that professional and corporate vitality in business might have a common root with the vitality of an organization that has a chapter in virtually every city in the nation. I wondered whether serving others had anything to do with their success.

"The movement started on June 10, 1935, with some help from the Oxford Group in England. They wanted us to become a select group, but we decided we needed to reach out and help everyone, without regard to individual background or origin. So we formed Alcoholics Anonymous out of the individual needs of all people who had hit bottom. Actually, it was just two people at first: A fellow named Bill and a friend from New York. Bill had been trying desperately to stay sober after many hospitalizations. Finally, his doctor gave up trying to find an answer, feeling that Bill was a hopeless case.

"There were others who were also concerned about the problem of drinking: One went to Switzerland and met with Carl Jung, one of the fathers of psychiatry. He came back, worked with Bill, and ultimately helped Bill stay sober, but that man didn't. But before that, the real beginning of Alcoholics Anonymous happened when Bill walked through the lobby of the Mayflower Hotel in Akron, Ohio, on his way to the bar. A deal that would have made him rich had just fallen through, and Bill felt deeply disappointed. A register of churches caught his attention, and he ran down the list until he saw the name of an Episcopalian priest. The priest knew of the problem and told Bill, 'If you can stay sober until tomorrow morning, I'll put you in touch with someone else who has the same problem. Maybe the two of you have something in common and can work it out.'

"The meeting took place the next morning in Henrietta Seiberling's gatehouse, on the grounds of the famous rubber family's estate. It lasted six hours. Out of this meeting came the beginning of Alcoholics Anonymous and the adoption of something called the four absolutes—really four principles that came from the Oxford Movement. They've worked for a lot of people over the years.

1. Complete honesty, or the ceaseless search for truth
2. Unselfishness, or thinking of someone else's need and not one's own need alone
3. Love, the medium of communication to others
4. Purity, or the unrelenting desire to do what is right

"These four absolutes from the Oxford Movement are foundation stones for a person's ability to serve completely. They mean a great deal to a recovered alcoholic, because an alcoholic has learned to do more than just say them. They come alive and make an impact on *you* when you put them to work in serving someone else."

"How did you become involved in this movement, Gene?"

"I was working on a special project for General Motors in 1939. We weren't in the war then, but we knew we would be. I was in the navy and landed in Chicago at the Old Midway Airport. It took me seven days to get to Evanston, and that's only twenty-five miles. That was the last drink I had. Someone brought me a few little pamphlets and asked me to go to a meeting on Saturday. I told him I'd go, but I began to feel better and later decided not to go, until a person came to my door that Saturday night. It was a fellow who had lived in my hometown. We grew up together, but they didn't know that when they sent him to pick me up. All he had was an address. That made a deep impression on me. I felt it wasn't just a chance that he was the one selected to pick me up. He had only been in Alcoholics Anonymous thirty days, and here he was already helping someone else."

I found that Alcoholics Anonymous puts a person to work helping someone else as soon as possible. The idea of serving someone else certainly had worked with Gene Cooper. In my view, Gene had learned how to be committed to other people's problems and needs so much that he had come to do it automatically.

Alcoholics Anonymous also uses a drawing similar to the seven attitudes I had uncovered in working with loss of vitality on the job (see Illustration 16).

The Progression and Recovery of the Alcoholic

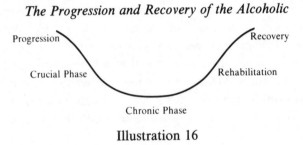

Illustration 16

The keys to vitality in the workplace and the solutions provided by Alcoholics Anonymous have similar roots, even down to a set of four absolutes for the alcoholic that help a person achieve one of the four steps to the committed attitude in business. Among the four steps I had used: to serve completely, to believe wholeheartedly, to recognize immediately, and to act decisively, I believe Gene had learned best the power of serving completely.

The more I listened to Gene Cooper, the more I began to see why he had recovered from alcohol addiction and was celebrating forty-five years of sobriety. Gene Cooper celebrates by helping everybody—his wife, Maggie, an invalid for years, now blinded from a stroke; a family on a Colorado highway with nothing left; and me, on the way to Cheyenne.

But what does all this mean to you? Gene Cooper's words carry even more insight than we've already discovered. In addition to the recovery power of serving others completely, Gene had mentioned the importance of Bill getting together with someone else to work through their recovery *together*. That is the same discovery I had seen in New Perspectives. You, too, can get together with someone else—in looking at your job, your organization, or your part of the recovery of America. Get out of yourself and get into helping out a person with a similar job problem or career concern or company issue. The act of serving someone else completely—or practicing your serve—can help you see new ways to become committed on the job. You can literally help yourself by helping someone else. But you've got to do it *for* someone else, not just for yourself, or you'll miss the message and the power. You've got to have a purpose that is beyond your personal gain alone.

But serving is not enough. You will need the power to believe in others. Next you will learn of a young woman at Navistar who is learning to believe in others as she helps revitalize the former International Harvester Company—from the inside out.

17

The Power of Believing in Others

The world is moved not only by the mighty shoves of the heroes, but also by the aggregate of the tiny pushes of each honest worker.

—FRANK C. ROSS

What do you do with an organization that began in 1831, with its roots in the agricultural heritage of America, and grew into an overconfident giant? International Harvester became too comfortable in its accustomed favorable agribusiness and medium and heavy truck market share. Its people saw little value in risk and little reason to do anything different in their enviable business enterprise. But what do you do when a five-year nightmare of crisis after crisis totally changes your

143

size, your market, your form of management, your company, and your beliefs?

In 1979, International Harvester had 97,600 employees. By 1985, that number had plummeted to 15,000, with their company roots pulled out of agriculture forever, after 154 years of harvest. But by 1985, International Harvester had also started to do something different, from the inside out. It had come from an idealistic attitude to a new awareness and decision. The winds of change in the worldwide capital goods markets and particularly in the midwestern world of agriculture had caused International Harvester to become one of the great business stories of the century as three chief executives and three presidents in four years desperately tried to revitalize the company. Now, with decisiveness, International Harvester looked for the way to become a committed organization, and a bright young woman is at the center of the activity.

Roxanne Decyk, in her early thirties, had responsibility, as senior vice-president for corporate relations, to help shape the revitalizing of International Harvester to Navistar International, a company that manufactures and sells medium and heavy trucks and diesel engines. Under the direction of Donald D. Lennox, chairman of the board, Roxanne, like her company, won't take the lessons of the past lightly—and she won't take the future lying down.

"What went wrong?" I asked Roxanne as she sat in her office over Chicago's bustling Michigan Avenue.

"There were several things," she responded, without a moment of hesitation. "We had followed a pattern of underfunding, for one thing. Our attitude was, 'We're okay,' and we might have been, but a six-month UAW strike in 1979 over work rules depleted our cash and forced us to borrow a lot of money. Then at the end of the strike, interest rates rose to twenty-one percent and not only destroyed the market for large equipment, but raised the cost of our debt. Low cash, high interest, and recession was the unbeatable trio of destruction, it seemed. We were even concerned that chapter eleven protection would be necessary. But now we are a focused company, we have a firmer financial foundation, and we are doing something about our organization."

Doing something different, a phrase I had used with individuals in the New Perspectives program elsewhere, was one of the answers for International Harvester as an organization.

Roxanne, an energetic young woman with analytical strength, insightful communication, and a sense of purpose when she talks, believed that management style was the answer to International Harvester's dilemma, and she wholeheartedly believes in the future of her company. But at the root of this belief is her belief in others. Not given to fuzzy thinking, Roxanne has a clear vision of the road Navistar (the "new" International Harvester) must take to stay out of the ruts of the past. And it's not a winding dirt lane, but a straight highway to a new way of managing based on belief in people. Looking for the impact of individual style on organization revitalization, I asked Roxanne, "What is your personal management style?"

"I believe that an attitude of high expectation in general results in high performance. At Navistar, we are identifying the longest-term objectives and goals that we can. And we're making them specific."

In Roxanne's view, the strategic framework of the organization must be widely and clearly understood, then an executive must practice a great deal of delegation. "You've got to trust the people you are working with, and you've got to let them participate with you," she said. "After you've studied and discussed things with the people who work for you, you've got to say, 'Go and do what is necessary.'

"This isn't easily accepted, though, when people haven't been operating that way. There is some skepticism in the middle and lower levels of management. Many who report to me were quite traditional, and they had to make a real adjustment to a younger woman as their manager. Some were hesitant to accept the scope of freedom and delegation I wanted everyone to have. I found that clear, simple directions were the key.

"The old style was, 'I'll tell you exactly what I need to know, and then I'll assemble the information and report it to my managers above.' My style is, 'I don't want to hear everything. I'm comfortable trusting you, as long as we've agreed on the expectations.'

" 'I only want to hear the problems and the results,' I told them. But I was surprised to see the unwillingness to take a risk." Roxanne's style of clear expectations and communication of problems fits in squarely with chapter three's idea of removing the gap between expectations and reality.

"We had to look at how we were managing the entire company," Roxanne continued. "And we tried to do it together. I'm enthused when I see a group looking at a problem together. The initial results are better that way, and the final implementation is improved, because people are already missionaries for the proposed solution. That's part of the value of getting honest participation. We spend less energy trying to sell people on a new approach when it's *their* approach."

As I thought of the rebirth of International Harvester, I realized all over again how important it is to consider people around you as your customers, even those who work for you, as well as your manager.

"How's it working?" I asked Roxanne.

"The old style may have been right for the times, but now the times are new. Now we have both younger and older people who are willing to risk something to encourage delegation. But not everyone is committed to this new attitude. Some people are 'changed out.' Some want to go back to the old way."

In mid-1985, International Harvester had as a senior management group, a chief executive officer, a president who was the chief operating officer, a chief financial officer, a general counsel, and a corporate relations officer. Roxanne Decyk directed corporate relations with 120 people, spread across human relations, labor relations, government relations, advertising, public relations and employee communications—along with people in corporate security and in corporate aviation services. I asked her, "What helped you get where you are?" Modestly, she told me she was in the right place at the right time.

"I guess there was some luck in all of that, but I did have wide experience that provided me with the confidence I needed to be willing to take risks. I have a hunger to explore new experiences. I resist deciding that I don't like to do something. I believe the individual outlook of a person frees up people in other positions around her."

Roxanne's belief in herself and others and her willingness to risk is her way of pushing out the walls of her job. One of her favorite questions has been, "I know we've had this policy for years, but why do we need to follow it now? Do we need that many signatures *now?*"

The power of timely, searching questions can change old ideas, and ultimately an organization, whether it's Navistar International or your own. However old an organization is, however well thought out its policies are for yesterday's problems, all organizations need to be challenged with relevant questions about current practice.

I asked Roxanne about the role of the individual in organizational vitality.

"I believe individual vitality is necessary among key members to inspire overall organizational vitality."

"But what are the characteristics of this vitality for you?"

"It's this hunger for exploring something new that I mentioned. And it's a sense of enthusiasm—a tendency to be enthusiastic about the potential around you and to bring your enthusiasm for potential smack into the middle of the organization. When you say to someone, 'I know you can do it. Try, and we'll all live with the results,' that attitude becomes contagious."

"What about Navistar's vitality?"

"We're involved in a fascinating experiment. In early 1984 we brought twenty-two officers together and identified the values of this company. Then we designed a program to gather all the ideas we could find on what it will take to be a successful organization.

Some thought what we were doing was hokey or idealistic, but others became deeply committed. In 1984 we sent the statement of our beliefs out. It was controversial. Some thought, 'This sounds like this year's fad,' and they kept their heads down, thinking it would pass over. That was before we began our negotiations with Tenneco that ended with our sale of the agriculture business.

"The timing of that sale didn't allow us to credibly say to our employees, 'We want to create an environment for career growth' just when we were selling a substantial part of the company to Tenneco. We were faced with the challenging task of refocusing our organization, with only fifteen thousand people left. But for those fifteen thousand we had to say, and mean it, 'We really do need new values. We really are committed to our employees. We really want participation and the creativity that grows out of it.' "

When I discussed with Roxanne the seven attitudes that can make or break an organization, she said, "We were idealistic. We've gone through frustration, defiance, and even resignation, but we've become aware. Now we're between decisive and committed, and it's going to take us some time."

Undergirding everything Roxanne said, in the spirit of confidence that seems a part of her, rests a wholehearted belief in herself and in the rightness of what she and her management team are doing at Navistar.

"If someone, even one person, is really committed to something, it is easier for others to catch enthusiasm."

"But how do you institutionalize this commitment, this belief in what you are doing?" I asked.

"First, by believing that we *must* institutionalize it. And we're going to do that through example and through training and education. That's our key. Right now, we are budgeting for education to institutionalize vitality in our organization."

"And behind all this, what do *you* really believe in?" I asked, searching for a statement of the purpose that motivated Roxanne.

"I feel we have identified a theme for change in this decade. The major currents in the United States in the sixties were created by legislation in the civil-rights and Great Society programs. In the nineteen-seventies there was a current of change through litigation, the enforcement of civil rights and environmental laws, for example. But the nineteen-eighties are the decade of change through the corporation. With more and more people working, with time spent on the job the most significant time commitment for most people—and our time commitments are staggering at times—we must move from cynicism to commitment. It's important for people at work to feel that this was a worthwhile week. The potential for success is so great that even some of America's organizations that were traditional to the point of orthodoxy are now encouraging new ways to work. There is a connection between financial and philosophical success."

Roxanne Decyk is really speaking about belief—wholehearted belief that there is a better way to work in America. But what does all this mean to you? Unless you believe in something—something workable and worthwhile—you may end up in an organizational rut. Like International Harvester, you may reach a point where all you have to believe in is belief itself. But one thing seems sure when you talk with Roxanne Decyk. Nobody there who put a hand to the plow will make it by looking back. People are now looking ahead. International Harvester has decided not to look at the plowed furrows of the past. To insure that, they even got rid of the plow. Now they are putting their belief in the people who can help them look ahead and they are doing it under a new name: Navistar, the rebirth of International Harvester.

In the last section of this book you will learn how organizations grow, decline and renew. You will learn about your own role in the coming decision crisis for business America.

Part IV

Recreating Vitality in American Businesses

18

The Need for Vitality Agreements

Men have never been individually self-sufficient.
—REINHOLD NIEBUHR

In the on-rushing pace of technology, with its obvious advantages but unrelenting international competition and mounting personal pressures, we need to know where we really are heading in American business. We need a new level of business vision balanced with an equal depth of personal comfort.

Erich Fromm said, "We may be at the crossroads of decision . . . how to improve the individual contribution toward the end that man avoids obsolescence and the country still succeeds in maintenance of its place among other countries as a viable force in the markets of the world."

It's not easy to put this kind of vision and action together for an entire nation when it is difficult to put vision and action together for just one organization. Edward Kappus and I talked about this. Ed is president of Management Strategies International, an organization with an international vision that is turning into reality after a surprisingly short time. Ed Kappus said, "An organization can't be vital unless senior leaders are vital. Usually more than one is needed. Organizations need a consensus of vitality—several people who can translate the mission of the organization with enthusiasm—people who can listen without prejudgment, who have no hidden agendas, who can share ideas without reference to roles." He went on to speak about business covenants and commitments that are emerging in organizations.

The Need for Honesty

The Young Presidents' Organization is an association of vital business entrepreneurs who have become president of their organization by age forty. The Young Presidents' Organization has an international program that fosters local forums, really small group covenants somewhat like those Ed Kappus described, where presidents meet in absolute commitment to confidential sharing of organizational leadership problems and personal concerns. Walter Green is chairman of the Harrison Conference Services, headquartered on Long Island and a member of a presidents' forum group. According to Walter, someone in his group can say, "I am afraid I can't be successful without my business partner, yet we are at cross-purposes. I don't know where to go or what to do."

This opportunity just to talk, to admit inabilities and weaknesses in the face of a crisis, is a help—so long as members are honest with each other and each is honest with himself. Members of these local forums are learning the practice of honesty together. But what about the need within a single organization as well as in an association of presidents who are equal?

As John Gardner expressed it, "The organization needs provisions for self-criticism. The individuals who hold the reins of power cannot trust themselves to be adequately self-critical. The danger of self-deception is very great; the danger of failing to see problems or refusing to see them is ever present."

All of us need to overcome the Ensign Pulver syndrome that we saw in the film *Mr. Roberts.* Ensign Pulver never wanted to see the ship's captain. The reason was that he had not faced himself honestly. This ability to be honest and to face others who may say something you don't want to hear is an exposure most people within an organization don't want to develop. But at the leadership level, wherever that is, people must have honest advice, and it must be *helpful* honest advice. In talking with people on sensitive issues, I have found this saying helpful: "People don't care how much you know until they know how much you care." This means that I will listen to almost anything you say to me about me, if I feel you are telling me something for my help. You can be honest with me if you care about me.

Jane Cahill Pfeiffer and I visited at her home in Greenwich, Connecticut. Jane was chairman of NBC, vice-president of communications and government relations at IBM, and a White House Fellow. I asked her, "What do you think is needed in today's corporate office?"

"An absence of ego," she said. "What you need at the top is the courage to stand up against all odds; you need a person who is painfully honest, but whom you respect. You need a blend of honesty and caring, and the ability to motivate by challenge, even though that may cause a dash of fear. I think to do that well you've got to develop the whole person. There are no easy shortcuts to this. What you don't need is arrogance at the top. That encourages prejudgment. Prejudgment turns off insights, and that affects the entire organization. Honesty without arrogance is a universal need of business."

"What about the organization?" I asked. "What prescription is there for the system itself?"

"The organization needs a clear purpose, measurable and attainable goals, and a system that supports ethical operation and the value of dissent."

The idea of honest dissent and considerate discussion that preserves respect for the person is a key to real consensus, and it can't be just honesty alone. Leslie Buckland summarized this well when he said, "If you're going to do your own barking, don't buy a dog."

A consensus of vitality must be built on honesty balanced with consideration. It sounds simple, but there aren't many who learn it well. Successful executives of the future not only *can* learn it but *must* learn it. The forums of the Young Presidents' Organization are establishing that. Career people at all levels need considerate honesty in order to become successful in handling the increasing pressure of international competition that will push us all into utilizing ever-changing complex technology. Whether or not we are ready for it, the pressure of change will come.

To get ready for the future, we must learn how to face new visions and new pressures with new ability to talk both honestly and considerately, and we've got to do that over a far wider base than we have in the past.

Is it better to make 40,000 middle-level leaders 10 percent more effective or 4,000 top level leaders 50 percent more effective? Either selection is good, but it's a better approach to say, "Let's try to do both." In time we may learn how to make 40,000 leaders 50 percent more effective. Then, instead of having an increase of effectiveness from 40,000 middle-level leaders to 44,000 or from 4,000 top level leaders to 6,000, we will have an increase of effectiveness among all 50,000 leaders throughout an organization without adding even one more person to the payroll.

Effective Management Assessment

A new approach to helping improve an organization's effectiveness has been developed by Worcester, Massachusetts, based consultants, Leo F. McManus and William P. Densmore. Their "Elements of Effective Management Assessment Process (tn)" enables a management team to look at how the team is performing against each of twelve elements of effective management. The approach provides balanced emphasis on all of these key elements and avoids the pretense of a quick fix based on the latest management fad. Densmore has provided the following extracts from the complete descriptions of each element that is a part of the assessment process.

The Twelve Keys to an Effective Organization

1. *INTEGRATED STRATEGIC MANAGEMENT:* A strategic management process defines the unit's mission and values, and creatively analyzes the business and its environment to arrive at winning strategies, results expected, and resource allocations. The process is integrated with operations and understood and accepted at all managerial and professional levels.

2. *FOCUS ON RESULTS:* Focus on results provides the key to unit effectiveness and to job satisfaction, encourages getting things done, and discourages bureaucratic busyness, procrastination, and perfectionism. Goals and measurements of progress provide "how am I doing" feedback at all levels.

3. *SHARED AIMS, VALUES AND BELIEFS:* The unit's broad aims and its guiding values and beliefs are clear to all. These understandings are a source of pride, and they generate teamwork and a sense of common purpose.

4. *SHORT-TERM/LONG-TERM BALANCE:* In management emphasis and interest in reward systems there is appropriate balance between short-term and long-term investments.

5. *SUPERIOR CUSTOMER SATISFACTION:* Superior customer satisfaction is recognized as a winning strategy, and is achieved through unit-wide commitment and attention to customer-satisfying products, services and attitudes. Quality is viewed as contributing to productivity.

6. *FOCUS ON PROFITS:* All are aware that profits (or economic viability) are a requirement for long-term business success. People relate this to their own security and opportunity. Productivity improvement is everybody's job.

157

7. *HUMAN RESOURCE PRACTICES:* People are a valued and respected resource. This is demonstrated by the behavior of managers, and reinforced by modern personnel practices for selection, performance expectations and review, personal development, salary administration, and information sharing, etc.

8. *FREEDOM WITHIN BOUNDS:* Managers provide as much freedom as each person's experience and capabilities permit, within broad bounds that they work out together. Performance objectives leave room for innovation. The authority of knowledge is more important than the authority of permission.

9. *HIGH EXPECTATIONS—FOCUS ON COMPETENCE:* There is an atmosphere and an expectation of competence and high performance. People who are not performing move to a more appropriate assignment in or out of operation.

10. *BUSINESS TEAMS AND TEAMWORK:* Cross-functional business teams are common, with team members committed to common business objectives, and with clear understanding of goals, roles and procedures. Collaboration and teamwork is the norm between functions and between line and staff.

11. *INFORMAL NETWORKS AND RELATIONSHIPS:* Managers and professionals recognize the importance of informal relationships, and use such networks to get things done with little formal structure.

12. *CLIMATE FOR CHANGE:* At all levels and in all units, a climate for change prevails. Innovation is highly valued, risk-taking is encouraged, and defending the status quo is questioned. Technology is up-to-date.

What thread can you use to sew these twelve elements together? Communication. Honest, considerate communication. Without it the elements don't knit together into the comfortable sweater that business needs. Beneath the business suit you are wearing you will need a warming sweater that keeps you and your organization from growing cold. That's what the Young Presidents' Organization is learning and what Ed Kappus refers to when he says, "We need a consensus of vitality." To achieve that in your organization, and in American business, we all need to learn how to be honest and considerate at the same time. One without the other won't work. With both, you can help your organization and business America break through to new togetherness that is sorely needed and will be absolutely critical to the future as technology rushes toward us at breakthrough speed.

19

Helping Your Organization Break Through

Once an organization loses its spirit of pioneering and rests on its early work, its progress stops.

—THOMAS J. WATSON

Organizations are like people. They are born with needs. They grow with ideas and decline with lack of vision. But, also like people, sick organizations can become revitalized and healthy again.

Some organizations become ill from lack of interest and nourishment, lack of flexibility and exercise, even lack of purpose—or all three. But one cause usually leads to another, and you can always find a prime cause.

Most organizations that die are guilty of suicide, whether or not those who committed it understood what they did. If you look close enough, you can actually see an organization follow the same seven attitudes that individuals follow. Organizations go from idealism to commitment just as people do, because they are nothing more than a body of people, and you can see when one has become resigned and headed for trouble.

In the 1930s a towheaded young boy used to wait at the end of his porch to see a sleek black Packard with white sidewalls and classic chrome grille whistle by. It was a window on an exciting world as the Packard appeared each afternoon for an instant, rounding the corner, flashing by the porch, disappearing down the hill, always hurrying. One day the Packard was late, and the little boy waited with growing worry, until he finally dashed into the house to ask his mother, "Did I come out too late?"

"No," she said. "Go back and wait. It will come by."

Finally, the Packard came, not speeding this time, but tilted up in the air behind a wrecker. You could see the crumpled grille and fenders as the crippled black beauty trailed the wrecker down the hill and out of sight. That was the experience of the Packard Motor Company, too. Nobody wanted the proud Packard to pass from the American scene. Managers just weren't looking for the danger signs that preceded the death of an organization that no one imagined would someday be gone. But Packard could have been saved. Was it lack of interest and attention? Lack of flexibility in the organization? Whatever the prime cause, Packard committed suicide, due in part to lack of vision for the future. The organization became too content with the comfortable expectation of invincibility in the marketplace. Packard was actually dead long before many saw it was ill from lack of vision.

Every organization needs three levels of vision. If it gets stuck with only one level and doesn't raise its sights to the second and third, it is already crippled, and it's just a matter of time before the wrecker comes by. Consider these for your own organizational vitality:

Three Levels of Organizational Vision

1. *The Do-able:* This is the most obvious level. If your organization never strives beyond the apparently do-able, it will lose its organizational exercise and muscle.
2. *The Conceivable:* If your organization goes beyond the do-able and allocates some time and energy to the conceivable, it will stimulate its mental muscle enough to create a climate for trying harder and will introduce an attitude of decisiveness.
3. *The Previously Unthinkable:* If your organization is willing to go beyond the second step to the point of actually *attempting* the conceivable, no matter how hard it seems, it is just a matter of time before the organization will raise its sights to the previously unthinkable, the most challenging level of all.

A vital organization must think on all three levels in order to become periodically reborn. And all organizations, like individuals, need the rebirth of ideas that cause new exploration, increased exercise of talents, and the discovery of previously unthinkable products that result. This same level-of-vision process works with individual vitality. If you haven't gone beyond your present idea of what is do-able for you, you will limit your personal vitality and the vitality of your organization—wherever you are placed within it. Even if you are at a project level, hidden well down in the organization, you *can* do something different. You can break out of the six project stages someone described with good-natured cynicism:

The Six Project Stages

1. Wild enthusiasm
2. Disillusionment
3. Total confusion
4. Search for the guilty
5. Punishment of the innocent
6. Promotion of the nonparticipant

To avoid this sort of decline in your company (and the decline is very real, even though it may not take this form), you'll need to control the forces that cause it. Let's take a look at what you can do.

Organizational Forces

Every company, corporation, group and individual faces three forces: anxiety, pain, and enthusiasm. You must face these organizational forces around you squarely, or they will wash over you and your organization and carry you away.

Anxiety

Managers used to think of anxiety as motivation. But beneath all anxiety is fear. While fear has been used for centuries to get people to do things in the short run, it reduces your effectiveness in the long run. Sooner or later it will cripple your organization.

Anxiety is nothing more than sustained fear brought on by indecision over which way to go. Even two *good* choices will cause anxiety if you don't take one road decisively. And when you or someone who works for you sits in the middle of an intersection, you or he will get run over, sooner or later. When even one person sits in an intersection he places the entire organization there, too. Many businesses have died at the crossroads.

Anxiety alone ultimately kills your organization, your decisiveness, and you. The solution is to reduce it.

Pain

Pain is something we all avoid, sometimes at all costs, but pain is a totally different force. Though you don't usually seek pain, pain comes to you in your organization when someone loads you up with too heavy a schedule or too heavy a demand. But when you work through a difficult task, you usually learn something new from your experience. Pain actually develops you, just as exercise does. And make no mistake about it, strenuous exercise is painful, but it is also good for you.

If I give you a job that is too big for you, I tell you something about my belief in you. If I give you a job that is too small for you, I tell you something about my *lack* of belief in you. Which pain do you want? What will you do with the painful experiences in your organization? When I hand you a big job and I say, "I'll stand beside you when the going gets rough," you will grow from your experience because pain develops you—whether or not you enjoy it. You can take the pain of the big job and use it for personal growth.

Enthusiasm

Without this third force in your organization, you won't be able to handle the other two. You don't need to be wildly or idealistically enthusiastic. Idealistic enthusiasm doesn't work for long and is destructive in the long run. You can't pretend you have enthusiasm for long. You can't paint real enthusiasm on your face. But if you've got it, you show it—and it helps you and your organization. Real enthusiasm ignites people, families, athletic teams, churches, and business organizations alike. Enthusiasm is an inner quality. What do you do with it? You get it—or you get out.

What Do You Do About These Forces?

Here's a simple diagram of what we've been considering:

ANXIETY / KILLS / REDUCE IT
PAIN / DEVELOPS / USE IT
ENTHUSIASM / IGNITES / GET IT—OR GET OUT

I'd like to share with you a step-by-step way for you to reduce anxiety, use the experience of the people around you, and allow enthusiasm to ignite your organization. Whatever your position, you can still use some of these steps right where you are.

To demonstrate, let's assume you've been called in as a consultant to an organization. Over a hundred years old, at one time it played a significant role in American life. Now it is modest in size, with a $13 million revenue each year and a $9 million investment portfolio, with land and buildings valued in the low millions. It is currently financially stable, but management has noticed a major product is declining in acceptance. The president recently announced he plans to retire at the end of the year. Everyone feels the organization is uniquely prepared for a new level of vision, but no one plan has ignited the board of directors, the corporate officers, or the employees. The organization drifts close to resignation, even with its healthy financial position. Ultimately, it will die of lack of purpose and vision if nothing else causes the death earlier.

What will you do as consultant? Here are four areas to focus on in helping this organization, or your own, to regain its momentum and live up to its purpose.

Four Areas of Focus to Revitalize Your Organization

1. Strategic organization purpose
2. Strengths, weaknesses, and commitment of the board of directors, the corporate officers, or the top executive level
3. Profitability, purpose, communication, and vitality of the work force
4. Communication of purpose, programs, and products to the public.

Within these four areas of focus ask yourself these twelve questions:

Focus 1: Strategic Organization Purpose

1. What is the vision and mission of this organization today?
2. How can we best achieve it now, regardless of how we did it before?
3. What exactly do we want to do and when?

Focus 2: Strengths, Weaknesses, and Commitment at the Top

4. What are the strengths and weaknesses in our organization?
5. What should the task and role of the chief executive officer, the chief operating officer, and the top executives be?
6. How can we match the *tasks* of management with the *skills* of management?

Focus 3: The Work Force

7. What employee skills do we need?
8. How can we organize the people best?
9. How can we best communicate the purpose of the organization to the total work force, so that everyone can see where he or she fits in?
10. What skill development and personal growth can we offer to the employees?
11. How can we best listen to new vitality ideas, from the bottom up?

Focus 4: The Public

12. What can we say to the public that will insure their trust and acceptance of what we have to offer?

You can use these questions in your organization at various levels. Recognize as you do you put into practice four essentials in causing the rebirth of your organization.

1. Letting people *see* your organization vision and purpose.
2. Making sure you have *strategic direction* toward your organization goals.
3. Maintaining your profitability and purpose from the *top to the bottom* of your organization.

4. Making sure the public sees how *valuable and unified* your total
   services are.

From these essentials your organization will receive the revenue it
must have to stay vitally alive.

Looking again at motivation, you are about to discover the third
side of motivation, beyond the first two sides explored in chapter
five. The three sides look like Illustration 17.

Three Sides of Motivation

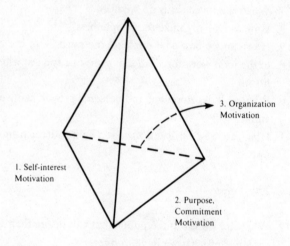

Illustration 17

Organization motivation depends on the self-interest and purpose motivation you examined in chapter five. The third side grows
from the combined motivation of all levels of people in the organization. Your organization becomes a more motivated force when
the management at the top establishes a strategic organization purpose and a set of beliefs that serve as a foundation for success. Your
organization becomes even more motivated when top management
looks at its own strengths and weaknesses honestly and becomes

committed to managing these realistically. Then when top management directs the work force toward gaining public trust and acceptance of its products and allows the real vitality of the work force to come through, the organization becomes a revitalized force.

The third side of motivation looks like Illustration 18.

The Third Side of Motivation

Public
Trust,
Acceptance

Vitality
of the
Work Force

Strengths and
Commitment
of Top Management

Strategic
Organization
Purpose, Beliefs

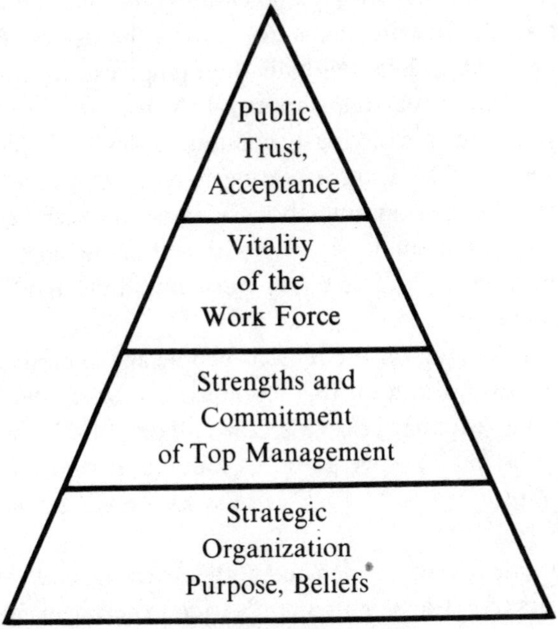

Organization Motivation

Illustration 18

Consulting with a number of organizations, I have found that the most effective are those that clearly understand and communicate the needs of their customers, translate these into clearly understood goals for the work force, and get out of the way so the people can do the work. When people are motivated by purpose and they know the right direction, they don't need someone looking over their shoulders. It's just as the old bowling analogy teaches.

Think of a bowling alley on a Saturday evening when the league is at the height of the season. What motivates all the people to work hard rolling a heavy ball down an alley?

Imagine you know nothing about bowling, and you arrive to observe league play. The alleys are packed with fired-up bowlers, but you have no idea why they are so enthused or what they are doing. Without letup, bowling balls roll down the alleys. Pins clatter against each other. Bowling balls thump against the cushions, and people constantly roar their approval or dismay. No one stops to look at you. They are obviously committed to their individual goals and to helping their team, sweating hard to give their best. To a stranger who knows nothing about bowling, the scene could be the second shift of a small factory, with automatic machinery constantly picking up and resetting pins. But there is no take-away product here.

You start looking for the reasons people are so motivated. "How much do they pay you for this?" you ask a bowler who has just returned to his seat after knocking down all the pins. Wiping his face, he says, "Pay me? You've got to be kidding. I pay to do this."

Why do people pay to work as hard as this all evening? you ask yourself.

You decide to rent an alley on another evening, and you advertise for bowlers to participate in a motivation experiment for an hourly salary rate. Now it's the evening of your experiment, and your hired bowlers are busy at work. But they begin to tire quickly as the evening goes on. Puzzled, you offer to increase the hourly rate if they roll the ball more often. Even then you notice that the activity soon slows down, so you try a few organizational solutions. You remove the distracting pins. In no time the bowlers are unhappy, and the ball rolling slows further.

Now you set up a curtain halfway down the alley, with a supervisor beside it to report how close the ball would have come if the pins were there. (If this sounds unrealistic, think of the role some supervisors play.) You tell the supervisor, "Use these positive recognition words if the bowler would have knocked down the pins and these negative recognition words if the bowler would have missed most of the pins." But soon you see that the bowlers are not motivated. You can hear their comments: "I know you said I'm doing fine [or that I missed], but by how much?"

Now you realize you need the pins, so you put them back, and you let the supervisor report as the pins go down behind the curtain. "Good job," he says.

"But how many pins are down?" the bowlers ask.

You can see this doesn't match the activity you saw on the first night you watched. Finally you remove the curtains and tell the supervisors to watch from the audience. Then the bowling enthusiasm picks up automatically. Why? Because people who know their purpose can improve on their personal skills and can help their team work harder, even if they pay for the opportunity. When management lets the goals be seen by everyone and each person has a chance to improve his skills, his satisfaction, teamwork, and productivity all go up.

Motivated organizations let people see the vision and the purpose. They make sure the employees know the strategic direction and the goals. They encourage everyone to participate in the purpose of the team, and they make sure that everyone can see the value of what each is doing for himself. Managers need to organize work so that it is naturally motivating and then get out of the way.

The bowling analogy you have just explored provides a key to organization motivation. No organization team will work well for long without the ability of the average team member to see the purpose of his or her effort—and how this helps get the real purpose of the organization achieved. Organizations are like people.

There are some final insights for you and for all business America. We've been overlooking them for years, and we can't afford to overlook them any longer. It's high time to draw on our real heritage, or we will all miss our highest opportunity. In the next chapter you will discover the fourth side of motivation—the bottom of the pyramid on which the three sides of motivation stand.

20

Decision Time for Business America

A man's main job is to become supremely aware of and intimately involved in the great issues of his time.

—SATURDAY REVIEW

In recent years, business America has become so preoccupied with the struggle for survival, successful competition, and excellence that we have lost our understanding of leadership. Our loss of vitality has shown itself not only in the declining quality of our products but in the lower quality of leadership that produces them. Nowhere is this more evident than in the way we make our decisions: We have emphasized the decision itself more than the process of the decision.

The *way* you make your decisions is more important

than *the decision,* because the steps to the decision can improve or destroy its result. Your *decision process,* not your decision alone, makes you a true leader in business. This is so important that it is now imperative to learn *not* to decide first, but to decide fourth. As a nation, as an organization, and as individuals, we must rediscover that the secret of national, organizational, and individual leadership is decision leadership. Examples of this already exist in history, but we have overlooked our heritage so long that we have lost our recognition of it. Now, even when we hear it or when we see it replayed in action, we don't recognize it for what it is. We are in danger of losing the fourth side of motivation, our real identity.

The Fourth Side of Motivation: Our Leadership Roots

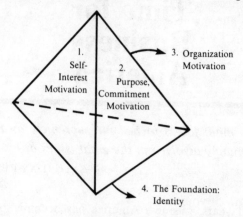

Illustration 19

A long time ago in another country, a great national leader died before reaching his goal of leading his people to a new land. A new leader assumed the task.

After the death of Moses, Joshua accepted the task of leading the first Israelites across the Jordan River into the Promised Land. Joshua was motivated by God's words when He said, "I say to you now the same thing I said to Moses. No one will be able to stand up to you for as long as you live, because I will be with you just as I was with Moses. I will not leave you and I will not fail to help you."

Serve and Obey Completely

"Joshua, I want you to be strong and brave. That way you will be a successful leader of My people, and they shall conquer all the territory that I promised to their ancestors. All you need, Joshua, is to be strong and courageous. If you obey to the letter every law Moses gave you—remember these are the laws I gave to him—you will be successful in everything you do. Never stop reminding the people about these laws, and you also must think about them every day and every night. I want you to be sure to obey all of them. Only then will you succeed. Remember what I say, Joshua. Be bold and strong! Banish all your fears and doubts! Keep reminding yourself that the Lord is *your* God and that He is with you wherever you go."

Moved by these strong words, Joshua sent a message to all Israelites, right down to the lowest in responsibility. "In three days we are going across the Jordan. We will conquer the people living there, and we will live in the land God has promised to us."

The people were motivated by Joshua's strong words of leadership and committed themselves to obey him as their commander-in-chief. "We will obey you, Joshua. Keep leading on with the courage and strength of your words."

When the third day came, messengers went through the camp, giving these instructions, "When you see the priests carrying the ark of God, follow them, but stay about a half mile behind them."

Believe Wholeheartedly

Then Joshua told the people "When the priests carrying the ark touch the water with their feet, the river will stop as though held back by an invisible wall!"

Normally the Jordan is not an imposing river, but it had been a rainy season, and the Jordan had overflowed its banks. As the people headed for the river, just as the feet of the priests carrying the ark touched the river's edge, far up the river the water began piling up as though there were an invisible dam. The water below that point flowed on to the Salt Sea until the riverbed was dry. Then the Israelites crossed, close to the city of Jericho. After a while the priests actually were able to stand on dry ground in the middle of the river, until the people passed over the riverbed.

The Israelites were so impressed by Joshua's decisive leadership that they trusted his direction for the rest of his life.

At the Lord's command, Joshua ordered the priests to come up from the riverbed. As soon as they came out, the water flowed again and overflowed its banks as it had before.

Recognize Immediately

Joshua ordered a stone monument built and told the people, "When your children ask you why this monument is here and what it means, tell them that these stones are a reminder of the miracle you have seen today."

Later Joshua was sizing up the city of Jericho, and a man appeared near him with a drawn sword. Joshua walked up to him and asked, "Who are you? A friend or an enemy?"

"I am the chief of the Lord's army," the stranger replied.

Joshua recognized that he was telling the truth and immediately knelt and worshipped him. "Give me your commands," Joshua said.

"Take off your shoes," the stranger told him. "This is holy ground." Again Joshua obeyed without further question.

Act Decisively and Creatively

Jericho had been securely guarded, because the citizens were afraid of the Israelites. No one was allowed to pass without strict clearance procedures.

The Lord said to Joshua, "I want you to march your entire army around Jericho each day for six days straight. Select seven priests to walk ahead of my ark, and instruct each one to carry a ram's horn trumpet. On the seventh day you and all your army must march around the city seven times. Make sure the priests blow their trumpets again. Then instruct them to give one long, loud blast and tell the people to shout as loudly as they can. When they do this, the walls of the city will crumble before them."

Joshua called the priests in and gave them their instructions. "I don't want to hear a single word from anyone until I tell you to shout. Then I want you to shout for all you're worth."

On the first day the Israelites carried the ark around the city once, exactly as they were told. The next morning they went around again as before. For six days they followed the same pattern to the last detail. At dawn the seventh day they started out again, but this time they went around the city seven times. In the seventh circuit the priests blew their trumpets long and loud, and when they stopped, Joshua yelled to the people, "Shout! The Lord has given us Jericho!"

When the Israelites heard the long trumpet blast, they shouted as loudly as they could. As the wave of shouts swelled around the city the walls of Jericho began to crumble and fall in front of them. The Israelites were lined up around the entire city, and they poured into Jericho from all sides.

This account of Joshua and the battle of Jericho, taken from the Old Testament, reveals a leader who served and obeyed completely, believed wholeheartedly, and recognized immediately, *before* he acted. It was the *process* of decision that made Joshua able to act so decisively and creatively. There was risk in his approach as there is risk in all decisions.

For you to make the big decision in your career, in your organization, and in your life, you must overcome the urge to decide first and learn to use the process of decision you have been learning in this book. The process is easy to understand but hard to make a part of our way of living. How does a totally new way of making decisions impact an entire community such as business America?

Joshua didn't have an easy time contemplating how he would look to an entire nation when he thought of how Israel might react to a command to walk up to the edge of an overflowing river. Suppose they refused? Further, what leader in his right mind would not be worried about his image if the river didn't obey? What leader in his right mind would not wonder when a complete stranger later said, "Take off your shoes," as they surveyed a city targeted for capture. What about walking around a fully defended city with armed enemy soldiers ready to hurl spears down on your entire army as you walk beneath them, unprotected, for seven days? Anywhere along the path around Jericho, Joshua's attitude could have turned from committed, back to frustrated. He could have asked, "Why seven days, Lord? Why do You want my entire army exposed?" Joshua could have turned defiant and resigned. But his commitment to serve, to believe, to recognize, and then to act, allowed him to continue in spite of any lurking doubt whether a huge city wall could be tumbled just by walking around it or by blowing a trumpet and shouting at it. Each day a wall looks bigger and more formidable, if you focus on the wall instead of your purpose. In your job or organization there are strong walls to scale and others to break through, and the walls don't appear to hold promise of comfortable rooms behind them. Unless you focus upon your purpose, all you can see is the wall.

Speak Your Way to Leadership

How does this kind of serving, believing, recognizing leadership start? It all starts with purpose and conviction that there must be a better way. The motivation starts with someone, somewhere, clearly saying what the purpose is. The power of saying or declaring your purpose is a commitment in itself. When Joshua heard the Lord say, "I am saying to you what I said to Moses . . . ," he heard conviction and commitment. He heard strong purpose and promise in the voice.

This way of speaking with total and unequivocable purpose is available to you. When you say to someone—when you declare what you believe or what you are absolutely committed to do—you will unleash the real power within your spoken word.

Have you ever seen a small woman stand up to a big man and declare her strength of commitment with her whole body and mind and heart? The power in the declaration itself is what the Scriptures refer to when they say "In the beginning was the word." This "word" is not just a selection of things to say. The word is the total living, creative, committed presence in the spoken word. So in a very real sense, you speak your way into true leadership as your resolve to serve, to believe, to recognize, and to act moves from your heart to your tongue to your actions. The process of commitment and of true leadership comes into being in the act of declaring, of saying with your total life presence what you will do.

Our Spiritual Heritage

This spiritual heritage is what will ultimately change American business life. The settlers of New England saw it. The Pilgrims and Puritans identified with the children of Israel as they crossed the Atlantic and settled in the New World with the "strangers" who came for business gain. Later the unusual combination of Puritans and entrepreneurs carried their sense of purpose into the Revolutionary War, when 70 percent of the Colonial Army was comprised of soldiers from Connecticut. When George Washington desperately needed help, Governor Jonathan Trumbull, of Connecticut, told his troops to remember their heritage as the new children of Israel, and they crossed the border into New York and helped defeat the enemy at White Plains. Strong business leaders have used similar strength of purpose and commitment to forge an industrial economy in America.

Your heritage is a spiritual, national, business, and personal heritage—a purpose and a presence that will carry you across streams, over walls, and into a new world of accomplishment you never thought available to you. However formidable your personal Jericho appears, it will surrender to your committed, declared attitude—or you will reach a point where you realize that it wasn't *your* Jericho. But how does this apply to business in America, and where do you fit in?

America is facing its own Jericho. The victory is not in strength of numbers or mental brilliance. We have worked our way into an American revitalization problem that must be resolved by the combined commitment of all of us. It is decision time for you, as part of business America. Assuming you already have ability, when you serve completely, believe wholeheartedly, and recognize immediately, you are ready to act decisively and creatively as a professional leader. Your part of business America will begin to recognize and someday to follow.

Now that you have finished this book you have reached a new beginning point for yourself, your organization, and business America. The question is not whether you *can* do the things discussed in this book, but *will* you? You are now at the threshold of breaking through.

Appendix

Appendix:
Breakthrough Forms

You may be interested in how to start your own breakthrough. To help you, here are several forms you can complete. The first several deal with individual breakthrough; the last two deal with organizational breakthrough.

Experience in revitalizing techniques shows that you are more likely to make changes when you write out the changes you want, in your own words. These forms provide you that opportunity. After using any of them you may wish to discuss them with someone you trust who has experience in business.

Personal Vitality Inventory

Date _____

Complete this and discuss it with someone you trust.

1. What purpose are you committed to as a person?

2. What is one thing you stand for and believe in as a person?

3. What is your real strength at this point in your life?

4. Do you have a personal goal to achieve or service that you want to perform in life—something that needs to be done or changed or eliminated? If you do, what is it?

5. Are you interested in a specific job, either in or out of your organization, that requires skills you do not possess? If you are, what is it? What specific skills does the job require as you now view it?

6. Do you have one or more skills in mind that you want to develop? If so, what are they?

7. How do you utilize the three steps—to serve completely, to believe wholeheartedly, to recognize immediately—to increase the power of your fourth step, drawing on the decisive power of purpose within you?

Attitude Inventory

Date _____

Consider three categories of your life—business, family, and personal—and place a circle on the attitude curve showing where you believe your attitude is now. Be honest with yourself. Next place an X where you would like your attitude to be on each of the three curves. Discuss these with someone whom you trust.

My Attitude in My Business Life:

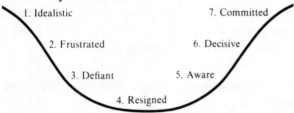

1. Idealistic   7. Committed
2. Frustrated   6. Decisive
3. Defiant   5. Aware
4. Resigned

My Attitude in My Family Life:

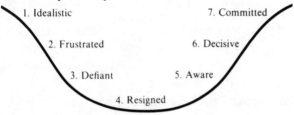

1. Idealistic   7. Committed
2. Frustrated   6. Decisive
3. Defiant   5. Aware
4. Resigned

My Attitude in My Personal Life:

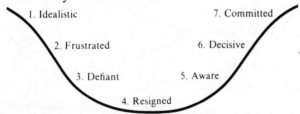

1. Idealistic   7. Committed
2. Frustrated   6. Decisive
3. Defiant   5. Aware
4. Resigned

Attitude Gaps

Date _____

The difference between your past expectations, the reality of your present circumstances, and your desires for the future can affect your attitude.

1. List below your past expectations, assessment of the present, and desires for the future.
2. Determine what changes you can make in your expectations, your present situation and your future by placing a checkmark by the item you could change.
3. Discuss these with a trustworthy friend.

For this circumstance:_____ (name an important present circumstance)

My past expectations were:

My present assessment of the situation is:

My desires for the future are:

The Four Sections or Rooms in Your Job

Date _____
Job Title _____

1. Fill in all your present job responsibilities you can think of. Enter them in the appropriate category below.
2. Next enter items that *should* be done to improve the impact of your job.
3. Discuss with management above you.

I	II
Relationship Responsibilities	Analytical-Judgmental Responsibilities
IV	III
Managerial-Administrative Responsibilities	Creative-Innovative Responsibilities

Four Steps to Professional Leadership

Date _____

To refine your professional leadership approach, examine these four commitments as you think of your present work situation.

As an individual:

1. These are the areas in which I am serving completely:

2. These are the areas that I believe in wholeheartedly:

3. These are the areas that I tend to recognize immediately (or presently):

4. These are the areas in which I want to act decisively and creatively:

Revitalizing Your Organization

Date _____

There are four focus areas that can help your organization become more vital. Use these questions as an individual, then ask selected people to complete them. Discuss them in appropriate meetings with selected individuals.

Focus One: Strategic Organization Purpose

1. What is the vision and mission of this organization today?

2. How can we best achieve it now, regardless of how we did it before?

3. What exactly do we want to do and when?

Focus Two: Strengths, Weaknesses, and Commitment at the Top

4. What are the strengths and weaknesses in our organization?

5. What should the task and role of the chief executive officer, chief operating officer, and top executives be?

6. How can we match the *tasks* of management with the *skills* of management?

Focus Three: The Work Force

7. What employee skills do we need?

8. How can we organize the people best?

9. How can we best communicate the purpose of the organization to the total work force so that everyone can see where he or she fits in?

10. What skill development and personal growth can we offer to employees?

11. How can we best listen to new vitality ideas, from the bottom up?

Focus Four: The Public

12. What can we say to the public that will insure their trust and acceptance of what we have to offer?

Organization Beliefs

The beliefs of an organization create its culture and cause it to maintain stability in varying economic, employee relations and strategic planning situations. With this in mind, consider the beliefs of your organization, whether written or merely implied by the past actions of the organization.

The beliefs of this organization are or seem to be:

The beliefs of this organization should be: